ARMED
&SMARTER

Advanced Concealed Carry
Weapons & Training

**David Bahde,
Paul Markel
& David Johnson**

ARMED AND SMARTER ≫

Authors:

David Bahde is a fulltime firearms instructor, tactical consultant and writer. His work regularly appears on Tactical-Life.com and in *Guns & Weapons for Law Enforcement*, among others. He wrote chapters 1, 8, 9 and 17 for this book.

David Hunter Jones has packed a pistol since legally able to do so. He's an avid hunter, shooter and outdoorsman and his work has appeared in Bassmaster and on OutdoorChannel.com, among others. He lives in Alabama with his wife, Carolyn and son, Hunter. He wrote various portions of this book. He wrote chapters 4, 9, 11, 12 and the Part I and Part II Introduction for this book.

Paul Markel is the host of the Sportsman Channel's series *Student of the Gun* and operates the Student of the Gun University training program. He has extensive military and law enforcement experience and now spends much of his time writing about firearm technique and safety for various publications. He wrote chapters 2, 5, 7, 9, 13, 14 and Part III Introduction for this book.

Providing Photography:

David Bahde, Terrill Hoffman, Craig Lamb, Paul Markel, Laurie Tisdale, National Shooting Sports Foundation, Hornady, Smith & Wesson and Viridian Green Laser

Cover photo by Oleg Volk

ARMED AND SMARTER

www.whitman.com

© 2014 Whitman Publishing, LLC
3101 Clairmont Road • Suite G • Atlanta, GA 30329

ARMED AND SMARTER
ISBN: 0794842062   EAN: 9780794842062

Correspondence concerning this book may be direct to the publisher.

Printed in the United States of America.

Basics encompass stance, grip and how you fire the handgun.

Running the Gun

Most shooters use the term "running the gun" to mean shooting a weapon until clearing all rounds from its magazine. The term also involves properly loading, holstering, drawing, operating and safely returning a gun to its holster. Thus, 'running the gun' encompasses all aspects of firing a gun from start to finish. In a shootout or competition, running a gun is all about keeping it loaded and operational. Because handguns operate on mechanical principles, shooters should familiarize themselves with how to clear malfunctions and best keep their gun operational.

The Basics

A shooter's ultimate goal is to accurately hit their target. Accuracy depends on a shooter's physical posture, focus and ability to align the sights of their gun. While simple in theory, accurate shooting demands shooters have complete control over both their body and mind. Most shooters will find the control needed to accurately shoot will only come after intensive, well-trained practice.

More specifically, a shooter must properly hold, aim and pull their gun's trigger to accurately fire their weapon. A shooter's stance and sighting can even influence their shot placement. Though no single method works for every shooter, most will find properly holding and aligning their gun's sights the key to significantly improving their marksmanship skills. It may take shooters some time on the practice range to determine what grips and stances best influence their accuracy.

Target acquisiton begins before pulling the trigger. It takes a proper stance, grip and knowledge of how the gun operates.

Running the gun involves loading, holstering, drawing and safely returning it to the holster.

Start with a stable stance that provides support for the pistol, balance and the ability to move.

Getting a Grip

A shooter's hands are the only part of their body that routinely contacts a gun when discharging rounds. Because of this, a good grip gives shooters the best control over their weapon and helps place shots on a target.

Most shooting experts would agree shooters' palms should make the most contact with their weapon as possible. Shooters should ideally use a two-handed grip, as both hands assist in aiming, trigger manipulation and recoil control of a gun. When firing a handgun, shooters should grip the gun tightly enough to properly aim and control their weapon, but loose enough to allow trigger manipulation. Experienced shooters first hold the grip with their dominant hand, then cup their support hand around the grip and their dominant hand. Ideally, your hands should cover the entire grip, while leaving some of the gun's butt exposed. We wouldn't recommend shooters place their support hand underneath their dominant hand or over a gun's butt, as this can compromise stability.

Once a shooter establishes a proper, comfortable grip, they can focus on aligning the front and rear sights of their weapon. After aligning the sights, a shooter can acquire proper sight picture. A sight picture is simply how one sees a target down their gun's sights, superimposing the sights where they wish the bullet to strike the target. When pulling the trigger, shooters should try to squeeze it in way that keeps their gun as steady as possible. If a shooter jerks the trigger when firing, they could pull the gun left or right and miss their target. Again, the way a shooter holds the grip and squeezes the weapon's trigger influences their accuracy.

The Stance

Stance remains one of the fundamentals of firing a weapon that new or intermediate shooters often overlook. While sight picture and aim are certainly important, all shooters should devote a fair amount of time developing a good shooting stance if they hope to improve their proficiency with a weapon. When preparing to fire, start with a stable stance that provides balance, support and range of movement. Without a proper stance, a gun's recoil could throw you off balance or compromise accuracy.

A good stance should help with balance when discharging a weapon. Stance needs to be wide enough to provide balanced support with a slight hip shift forward. Most, if any, handguns won't interfere with balance. Keep the shoulders and hips square to the target when using a fighting stance. This stance also helps absorb recoil and allows for rapid movement between or after shots. While some experienced shooters may prefer various stances, no single method works for everyone. If caught in a shootout, a good stance can also help to quickly flee from an attacker. Life-threatening situations may disrupt stance, so learn to maintain balance on the move.

When discussing the term "mindset," shooters often pair it with the words "combat" or "tactical." While every human with conscious thoughts uses some type of specific mindset every moment of the day, shooting requires a very specific frame of mind.

Certain tasks require different parts of our brains. Like the most detailed tasks we encounter, shooting demands an individual's full attention, requiring the analytic, sensory and discretionary portions of our minds. Because of potential dangers of neglectfully handling a weapon, a shooter should clear their mind before handling a weapon to avoid error. If an individual is particularly flustered, irritated or worried, we wouldn't recommend he or she handle a firearm.

Life-Saving Mindset

Read and study this chapter with a positive mindset. Before using a firearm, a new shooter should recognize their mind governs all their actions and inactions. With a positive outlook, a shooter will likely feel more confident firing their weapon and thus increase his or her accuracy with a weapon.

In a training course, the class might spend time on shooting mechanics, which is the physical skill of shooting. The class might also discuss the use of cover, carrying spare ammunition and carrying a backup weapon, which shooting experts refer to as tactics. You might further discuss your choice of guns, ammunition, holsters and flashlights or what is often called gear.

While shooters should thoughtfully consider each of these aspects, mindset alone determines how one can discharge a weapon and protect themselves if needed. Many law-abiding citizens choose to carry concealed weapons in public. While a concealed weapon can defend a person from an attack, those with their carry permit should ensure they have the proper mindset and confidence before carrying a loaded weapon. If a permit carrier doesn't have the right mindset, they might not effectively use his or her weapon against an attack. Because of this, some permit carriers may need to seek professional training to improve their confidence level with the weapon.

Your mindset determines if you seek professional training and then practice.

Combat Mindset

From a very specific point of view, the readers of this chapter will most likely take interest in the discussion of the "combat mindset." Let's examine combat mindset as two parts.

The following paragraphs require more than a mere cursory glance. Engage the analytical side of the brain, stretch thoughts and make room for new ideas. Consider what you may not have thought of before. You'll grow as a shooter and as a person by engaging in activities you've never explored before.

Willpower is using whatever tools or skills you acquire to defend your life and that of others, even if it means using deadly force.

Part One: Willpower

Mindset divides into two main areas: willpower being the first. Your willpower chooses the tools or skills required to defend your and others' lives, which may require deadly force. Here's an example of how willpower can influence a person during a difficult situation:

During an instance in Dayton, Ohio, two police officers responded to a domestic violence call that had devolved into an active shooting scenario. A deranged man was walking around the neighborhood randomly firing at anyone in sight. The officers exited their cruiser, used it for cover and confronted the man. When ordered to drop his rifle, the felon ignored the command and leveled his gun at the officers, demanding they drop their weapons instead. One of the

officers told the criminal she would talk with him rather than shoot. She came out from behind the car, set her gun down on the street and knelt down.

Unimpressed by her gesture, the felon walked up to the officer and shot her through the neck. Seeing his partner get shot, the other officer snapped out of his apprehensive fog, leveled his gun and shot the felon. The police quickly arrested the assailant, who survived his wounds to serve time in prison. Unfortunately, the officer shot through the neck would spend her next two years in a wheelchair, paralyzed from the chest down.

While the police officers could have justified shooting the assailant upon arriving on the scene, they instead hesitated. While their

intentions were honorable, they didn't enter into the proper combat mindset to help neutralize the threat. Even though these officers went through extensive training, they didn't do whatever was necessary to protect themselves and others. In retrospect, the officers likely wish they had swiftly and effectively shot the attacker rather than attempt to reason with him.

Owning a firearm or any other defensive tool and even practicing with it at the range does not impart the ability to use the weapon during a life or death confrontation. Mindset is 10 times more difficult to teach than marksmanship. While shooters should practice marksmanship, they also should ensure they have mentally prepared themselves to neutralize an attacker if necessary.

Part Two: Awareness

Awareness stands as the next most important aspect of a shooter's mindset. Jeff Cooper, the famed handgun expert and promoter of the "combat mindset," referred to awareness as "Condition Yellow." Condition Yellow is the situational awareness you should have for the world around you. After getting trained and obtaining a concealed carry permit, it won't do you much good if an attacker surprises you. To best defend yourself, you should try to anticipate an attack by staying alert to your surroundings.

Many shooters define situational awareness as being aware of what's happening in your environment. Simply, what's going on around you? Not just in front of you, but to the left and right and even behind you. In drivers' education, you learned to frequently check the rearview mirror for oncoming traffic. During defensive driver training in the police academy, candidates go through a series of mirror checks, which include rearview, left, right and back to the road. In civilian life, the repetition of that exercise keeps you constantly aware of what's going on around you. This kind of situational awareness results in near misses instead of collisions.

Cell phones and other electronic devices can easily demand your attention. While great tools, the attention cell phones require may cause you to ignore your surroundings. To prove how easily cell phones can distract a person, go to the mall or shopping center and watch people. How many people pass right by you with their heads down in their phone? Could you reach out and tap them on the shoulder before they would notice you? Could you attack them, grab a purse, knock them to the ground or otherwise assault them? While you may watch people for insight, criminals often target and attack distracted individuals. To avoid an attack, remain mindful of your surroundings and note those who look as if they're planning on harming or assaulting another person. People with their concealed carry permit have defused countless assaults by simply noticing those in their proximity.

Parting Thoughts

Having a combat or fighting mindset demands mental discipline. While some may succumb to the stress of an attack, you must decide that you will survive an attack if ever faced with one. While you can't decide or know when an attack could occur, you can decide if you'll survive one before even leaving your home. The decision to survive requires you take active steps to observe your surroundings and carry your weapon.

While we certainly wish innocent people never fall into harm, those who find themselves unprepared for an attack often do so because they haven't prepared themselves to fight for their lives. If you've taken the legal steps to carry a weapon in public, you must prepare for trouble and act accordingly if it ever arises. Again, while using a firearm in self-defense may seem daunting, training or reading additional books such as this one will help prepare both your conscious and subconscious mind for such event.

3: Basic Shooting Technique

Follow the basic shooting fundamentals when fine-tuning your shooting methods.

A pyramid can illustrate shooting fundamentals. Like the famous pyramids in Egypt, the foundations of shooting support its pinnacle or top. While briefly mentioned in the beginning portion of this book, the following chapter will further detail how you as a shooter can improve your fundamentals with a firearm.

Most shooting techniques taught today are variations of simple principles. While different shooting schools and training programs have their strengths and weaknesses, most instructors and experts base their curriculum off simple processes.

Many experienced gun owners and shooters vary their handgun techniques around their different applications. While infrequent, certain situations may require you to engage your gun in a different manner. Most popular shooting techniques will prove effective, but none provide the universal solution for shooting a handgun.

No single method works for everyone, as people come in all shapes and sizes. Strength and athleticism varies with age, so you should adopt the techniques best suited to your physical condition. Although advanced techniques vary, the basic fundamental principles remain unchanged and should form the basis of every shooter's foundation.

Two-hand grips need as much contact between hands and gun as possible.

The Grip

For the average shooter, the better the grip, the better the accuracy. While most experienced shooters develop slight nuances in their grip, the techniques in overall contact, thumb position and tension largely remain the same. This proper grip gives shooters the most control over their weapon. Two-handed grips need as much contact between the hands and the gun as possible. As mentioned, the dominant hand should rest high on the gun's grip, much as one would shake another person's hand. The middle, ring and pinky finger should secure the gun into your palm with enough tension to firmly hold it in place. After the dominant hand is in place, cup or wrap your support hand around your dominant hand, making as much contact with the grip and frame as possible. When doing this, ensure no space remains between the hands and the grip.

When holding a handgun, keep both thumbs forward pressing them flat against the gun's frame so they touch but not overlap. Those shooting 1911-model pistols with a thumb safety should rest the dominant thumb on top of the safety. Point your

Cross your thumbs and point them downward when gripping large revolvers.

thumbs forward if your gun doesn't feature a safety. While some make slight variations to their grip, make sure you don't point your thumbs up, backwards or down.

Those shooting a revolver will need to adapt their grip to their weapon. Like when shooting a semi-automatic pistol, you should hold a revolver high on the grip in a way that gives you firm control over the weapon. Revolvers feature a small gap where the gun's cylinder aligns with the front and rear of the frame. Though no real danger, gasses, powder, flame and even bullet frag-

ments can escape through this small gap when firing rounds. Because of this, try to keep your hands clear from the gap and below the cylinder.

Older guns and revolvers with powerful cartridges have a greater chance of letting gas and sparks pass through the gap in their frame. Again, while unlikely to severely burn your skin, point your thumbs down when firing large caliber revolvers, as this will help avoid minor nicks and burns. When shooting a small revolver, you may have to cross your thumbs along the side of the grip.

The Aim

Aiming consists of sight alignment and sight picture. Sight alignment involves leveling your gun's front and rear sight to your intended target. Front sights are generally square and look like a blade when viewed through the rear sights. Rear sights generally have a squared notch cut in the middle and may have two dots for visibility.

When aiming, focus your eye on the gun's front sight. Look for the sight at the end of the slide or on the end of the barrel furthest from the hammer. Keep your focus on the front sight as you look through the rear sight, letting the rear sights become blurry. Line up the front sight so it centers inside the notch or dots of the rear sight. Ideally, the tops of both sights should sit flush to one another. If the top of the sights aren't flush, you haven't yet leveled the gun.

Sight picture is the shooter's complete view of the target through properly aligned sights. Methods differ as to what shooters should keep in focus when aiming, as some prefer to focus on the front sight and others, the target.

Sight-focused aiming involves keeping the front sight in sharp focus and the target or threat blurry. Sight-focused aiming provides the best way to learn proper marksmanship and group shots on a target. Many small or distant targets require this type of aiming.

Threat or target-focused shooting places the threat in crisp focus while the front sight remains blurry. You generally get on target faster, but sacrifice precision. While shooting doesn't always require extreme precision, in a self-defense scenario solid hits and quickly firing could save your life. One should only consider applying threat-focused shooting after reaching proficiency at basic marksmanship. It is particularly advantageous with multiple threats.

With unsighted (or reflexive) fire, you don't use your sights when shooting at a target. In a self-defense or home invasion scenario, an attacker could strip your weapon from you if it isn't held close to your body. These situations may demand your weapon stay close to your body when firing at a target. While not as accurate as target or sight-focused aiming, you can align your sights in the direction of your oncoming attacker based on their proximity. Shooters use this tactic if they are on their back, pressed against a wall or if surprised and attacked in very close quarters. While you should never use this as your primary firing technique, it could work well within close quarters.

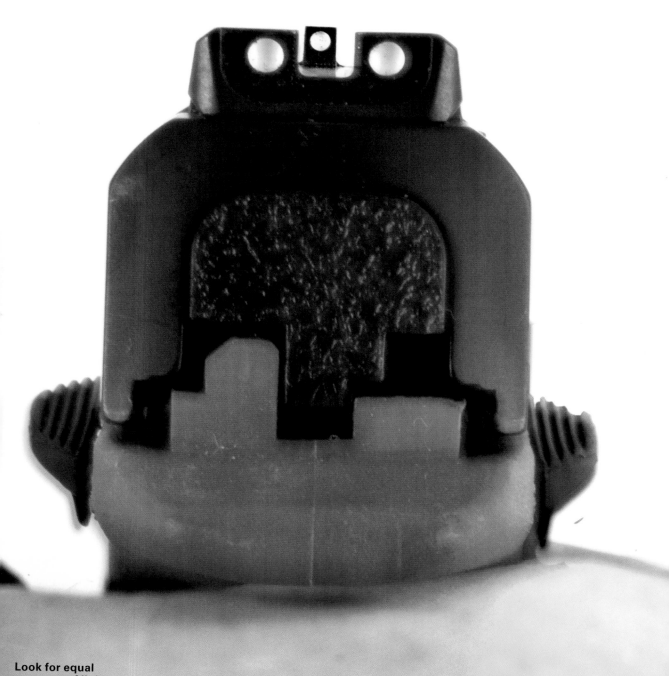

Look for equal amounts of light on each side of the front sight while visible through the rear.

Accuracy

You can assist your accuracy and precision by pressing the trigger straight back without pulling to either side. Squeeze the trigger with steady and even pressure until the pistol fires. A trigger's pre-travel (or slack) varies by the gun's make and model, so familiarize yourself with your weapon before carrying in public. Single-action pistols typically have less pretravel than striker-fired pistols, which demand shooters take up the slack by pulling the trigger back further before the striker engages and fires the gun. These striker-fired triggers move freely until they reach a specific point, when a slight increase of pressure will fire the weapon.

Double-action pistols and revolvers have no perceptible pre-travel but a long, heavy trigger pull. When shooting these guns, apply steady pressure to the trigger throughout the entire trigger pull. Double-action/single-action (DA/SA) pistols have a heavier pull on the first shot, while subsequent shots fire in single-action with minimal pre-travel. Most will find they shoot more accurately with handguns that have a light trigger pull and minimal pre-travel.

Shooters can achieve precision and accuracy with very heavy revolver triggers, but this requires significant practice to master.

After pressing the trigger and firing the weapon, keep the trigger pressed through the weapon's recoil. Then, slowly release the trigger until the sear resets while re-acquiring proper sight alignment and sight picture. Usually a shooter can feel or hear the click of the sear reset within their weapon. Once the sear clicks, a weapon can fire its subsequent rounds. Again, you don't need to fully release the trigger to fire your weapon, but just enough so the sear can reset. Either way, stay in contact with the trigger, take up the pre-travel (or slack) and prepare for the next shot.

During the firing process, each trigger press requires you to again find the sight picture. Practice this process slowly, as timing can determine the difference between accurate and poor shooting.

Accuracy comes by pressing the trigger straight back. Use just enough steady and even pressure to fire the pistol.

The Weaver is a shooting stance and technique valued for giving the shooter a solid stance and firm grip on the gun.

Stance

Stance supports your grip when firing a weapon. A good stance will allow you to properly aim, squeeze the trigger and absorb your gun's recoil. Stance contributes to how you apply pressure in your gun's grip. While plenty of different stances exist, most involve the same basic techniques.

When shooting, your stance should help keep you balanced and mobile. For a good, sturdy stance, place your feet at least shoulder width apart, giving you strong support. Also, keep your toes pointed towards the intended target with your dominant foot slightly behind the other. As you begin to fire, slightly shift your hips forward with your weight, but don't hunch. Keeping your weight slightly shifted forward will help absorb recoil and prepare you for the next shot. Standing up straight or with your knees locked will likely cause your weapon's recoil to throw you off balance.

Once you have taken the proper stance, you can acquire sight picture and sight alignment, as previously mentioned. To test your stance, extend your gun and aim as if to fire, but then close your eyes. After a few moments, open your eyes again and determine if your handgun moved from the target. If it did, you'll likely need to develop a sturdier stance for better balance.

Among others, sportsmen and gun enthusiasts have favored the Weaver Stance for decades. This stance involves fully extending the dominant arm and slightly bending the support arm. When doing this, the support arm should pull back as the dominant arm pushes forward to create tension between the gun and the shooter. Added tension develops by using the elbows or chest to create pressure against the sides of the pistol.

Creating this tension between the gun and the shooter should minimizes a gun's muzzle flip after firing a round. Various stances apply more or less tension to the gun, but every good stance should apply enough tension to control recoil and keep your grip intact. Practice various scenarios to find out which stance works best for you.

One step in drawing is staging the opposite hand on your belt or chest, preparing to add it to the grip.

Drawing and Holstering

Holstering becomes easy after learning how to properly secure any retention straps or other security features. Most should find drawing equally as simple. Various methods employ different steps on how to draw a weapon, but most involve some basic fundamentals.

First, get a solid grip high on the gun and release any straps or safety mechanisms on the holster. When doing this, stage the opposite hand on your belt or chest, preparing to place it on the grip. Pull the pistol up, clear the barrel and bring the gun up toward the threat or target. While extending the pistol forward, bring your support hand up to the proper grip position on the weapon. At this point, your weapon should be in the ready position.

Throughout this process, keep your trigger finger outside the trigger guard and up against or near the slide. Once you align your sights and prepare to fire, bring your index finger to the trigger and squeeze to discharge the weapon. When drawing your handgun, guarantee you have a clear view of your intended target and your index finger stays off the trigger until you've cleared the weapon from its holster.

After firing your weapon, remove your finger from the trigger. Returning the pistol to the holster simply reverses the steps. If there is a manual safety, then activate it prior to holstering. The same is true for a de-cocker device. Typically, the hammer should be down prior to re-holstering on pistols with de-cockers, although variations exist in certain devices and carry methods.

Press the magazine release to drop it. Bring the pistol toward the chest. Grab a fresh magazine using the opposite hand.

For a revolver, open the cylinder and hold it in the opposite hand. Use the same hand to turn the barrel up. Push the plunger down with the strong hand to release the casings.

Reloading

Many shooters use speed and tactical reloading when running their weapon. Perform either of these reloads with your gun close to your body and below eye level. When reloading, avoid pointing your weapon's barrel at any unintended target. The reloading process will differ with revolvers, but the same basics apply.

To speed reload a semi-auto pistol, fire all the rounds from the magazine currently in the gun. On an empty magazine, the gun's slide should lock to the rear of the gun, exposing the action. Once the slide locks into place, eject the empty magazine with your dominant thumb then insert a fresh, pre-loaded magazine back into the gun with your support hand. To successfully speed reload, you'll need to have multiple loaded magazines on hand to feed into the gun once you empty the other magazines.

Speed reloading a revolver requires a special reloading tool, typically known as a speedloader. Revolver shooters employ several reloading techniques, but the following demonstrates one popular method. After firing all the rounds in a revolver,

open the cylinder and hold it in the support hand. Use that hand to turn the barrel up. Push the plunger down with the strong hand to release the casings. Rotate the revolver barrel down using the opposite hand. Then, you must place the speed-loader over the revolver's empty chambers. If you've properly aligned the speedloader and the gun's chambers, the fresh rounds should fall into place. While speed reloading may prove more difficult with revolvers, with practice you should pick up how to quickly empty and insert new rounds.

Tactical reloads usually occur during a pause in a firefight or intensive shooting scenario. You'd perform a tactical reload if unsure how much ammunition remains in your gun. Like during a speed reload, remove a partially empty magazine from your gun and exchange it with one fully loaded. Most would find a tactical reload necessary in combat situations, when needing as much ammunition in the gun as possible at all times. When shooting on a range or for fun, most will not need to reload or replace their magazine before firing all of its rounds.

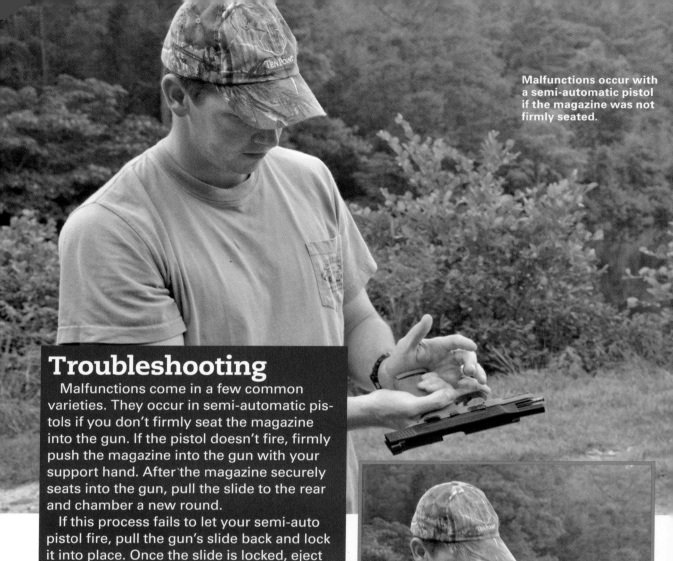

Malfunctions occur with a semi-automatic pistol if the magazine was not firmly seated.

Troubleshooting

Malfunctions come in a few common varieties. They occur in semi-automatic pistols if you don't firmly seat the magazine into the gun. If the pistol doesn't fire, firmly push the magazine into the gun with your support hand. After the magazine securely seats into the gun, pull the slide to the rear and chamber a new round.

If this process fails to let your semi-auto pistol fire, pull the gun's slide back and lock it into place. Once the slide is locked, eject the magazine, ensure the action and barrel are free of debris and re-insert the magazine into the gun. After loading a round into the chamber, try to fire again. If the gun still fails to fire, you may need an experienced gunsmith to repair your weapon.

If your revolver malfunctions or doesn't fire, press the trigger again to fire a new round. Ammunition can cause malfunctions, so a new round may solve the issue. Again, you may need an experienced gunsmith to repair your revolver if it fails to fire with new rounds.

Part II

The Well-Heeled Handgunner

Some gun owners find new handguns comparable to base model of vehicles; options abound of how to enhance your model. This chapter takes a look at firearm components and parts that could make you more effective with your handgun.

Aiming devices have come a long way since the six-shooters of the Old West. Many shooters now use laser sights and high-end competition guns no longer alone use red dot sights. Lights attached to the bottom of your weapon can now illuminate the darkest alleys. Every day citizens are packing these high-tech solutions for better handgunning and carry options have expanded as well.

The era of gunslingers and ammunition bandoliers have long disappeared. Modern plastics have revolutionized holsters for both law enforcement and civilians. You can comfortably pack a full-size 1911-style pistol under most thin coats.

While additions and modifications to your gun can improve your shooting, remember no magic accessory can substitute for training or spending time on the range.

4: Handgun Sights

Keep your eye on the front post and the rest will follow.

Few skills trump sight mastery on the road to becoming proficient with your weapon. Sights are to a handgun what a steering wheel is to your car. You see where you want to go and you point the vehicle in that direction by manipulating the wheel. When driving, you try and keep your vehicle on the road, which requires constant input and a steady hand. You need an even greater level of focus if you want to hit the bullseye or confront a threat with a handgun.

To many individuals, driving sounds simple: stop, go and turn. Once you get some miles under your belt, driving becomes second nature. However, mastery does not come without swerving off the road or running over a few speed bumps along the way. In handgunning, proper use of the gun's sights requires proper technique and familiarity with the sight picture. Shooters achieve mastery through repetition while encountering a multitude of scenarios. Just as a 16-year-old will not outrace Dale Earnhardt Jr. around Daytona, you'll not become an expert shooter without years of practice.

Second to the trigger, a gun's sights are its most important feature and learning how to properly use both will benefit your shooting.

Sight Knowledge

Most handguns feature open or iron sights, named so because blacksmiths originally forged sights into the metal of the gun. The term "open" simply means there is no tube or aperture to look through, like those found on a scoped rifle. The sights are out in the open. Most shooters find open sights ideal for handguns, as locating the sights is often easier. The sights have considerable distance between the sights and the shooter's eye, however they somewhat compromise accuracy. Precision target pistol shooters rarely use open sights and instead prefer precision or aperture sights. Speed shooters, however, rely on open or hybrid sights because of their good tactical and defensive options.

Before a shooter can successfully use any type of sight, they need to know which of their eyes is dominant. To test this, first point at an object across the room, and then close one eye at a time. If, when you shut your left eye and your finger is still on target as you look out

of your right eye, you're right-eye dominant. If, when you shut your right eye and your finger is on target as you look out of your left eye, you're left-eye dominant. You want your dominant eye to handle most of the work because it should lead and focus on a target.

For those planning on carrying a concealed handgun, examine how and where you plan to take your weapon. Though accurate and easy to aim, optics or scopes are often too large to properly conceal. Standard scopes also struggle working well in low lighting, where one would likely need to use their concealed weapon. Because of scopes' size and limitations, most of those who carry concealed weapons will prefer to use their weapon's barely-there notch-and-post sights. Shooters can choose from a variety of different types of handgun sights.

Knowing how your sights work is paramount for success in hand-gunning.

30

Night sights

Though the title may imply they give you eyes in the dark, night sights are merely highly visible dots that glow, thanks to tritium. Tritium is a radioactive gas that slowly decomposes inside a tiny vial. As tritium expires, it glows a greenish color. Tritium is radioactive but it is not dangerous. Trijicon and Meprolight are the big hitters in the night sight market. The dots glow continuously, but shine in complete darkness. You can still acquire a proper three-dot sight picture even in the dark. They are slightly more expensive than fiber optic sights and will fade over time, but most last a decade or more before a noticeable drop in brightness occurs. Both fiber optic and night sights are options on guns that have removable sights. Your granddaddy's single-action Colt with the sights machined into the frame is not the best candidate for a high-tech upgrade.

Night sights, like these from Trijicon, have tritium gas-filled tubes inside of them, making them glow. These are the best option for low-light shooting. This is a standard three-dot configuration.

Tritium is a radioactive gas that glows for several years before fading.

35

Two dot

A variation on the three-dot sight is the two-dot sight. As the name implies, there are two dots. Rather than lining them up horizontally, the shooter "stacks" them. Heine's Straight 8 sight is the most common example. When the two dots are touching and vertical, you are on target. Some consider these sights less complicated than three-dot sights since you are dealing with one less dot. Sights are simply a personal choice.

The two-dot system works well for some because of its simplicity; simply stack the dots on top of one another and you're perfectly aligned.

The ghost-ring sight provides a wide field of view for fast target acquisition, even in low light conditions.

Ghost-ring

Ghost-ring sights are a somewhat new introduction in the world of hand-gun sights. This aperture-ring style of sight is popular because it obscures less of the target when properly used. The rear sight is a large aperture (ring) that usually has a dot at the 9 and 3 o'clock positions. Once you peer through the aperture and find the front post, your eye is inclined to center automatically, theoretically ensuring a properly aligned sight. Ghost-rings combine the speed of a large aperture sight and the accuracy of a three-dot. The dots are often night sights, further-ing expanding their usefulness.

Aperture sights

Aperture sights can be slow to acquire, especially if the shooter is not familiar with them, but once you're comfortable with them, they're highly accurate. The adjustable rear sight is large and can be somewhat fragile, which precludes them from many serious defensive handguns. These sights are favored on target pistols that have long barrels and hair triggers, but die-hard peep sight shooters will accept nothing less. The smaller the aperture, the harder it is to use. The human eye is inclined to center the front sight within the rear aperture, which on paper makes for a more accurate shot. If you like looking through an aperture, strongly consider the ghost ring.

Aperture sights are popular on rifles and long-barreled competition handguns. They require a high degree of precision and practice to gain proficiency. In other words, they're very accurate, but they're more difficult to master.

Adjusting the sights

Most handgun sights are adjustable, but at the same time most do not need adjusting from the factory. Previously we talked about windage and elevation. Windage is the left-to-right aiming of a gun (think of the way the winds blows; horizontally), and elevation refers to the up-and-down aiming. Most handguns — especially semi-autos — have adjustable rear sights and higher-end guns and sights offer an adjustable front sight. Revolvers are a toss-up, as they sometimes have the rear sight machined into the frame of the gun, leaving only the front sight able to be adjusted, or vice versa. Rear sights that are adjustable most often are dovetailed into the gun, which offers windage adjustment. A small screw in the center of the sight will allow for elevation changes.

Many shooters get turned around when trying to adjust the point of impact of a bullet that's consistently not hitting the desired target. If you're sure of your setup, point of aim, and are positive that you're not flinching or "pulling" the gun as it goes off, your sights may need adjusting. Before adjusting the sights, though, try shooting it off of a rest first and see if you can duplicate the errant grouping. If the gun goes back on target, the culprit may be the Indian rather than the arrow.

If your sights are truly out of alignment, however, they need some attention. Here are the guidelines for adjusting the sights:

» To move the point of bullet impact up, raise the rear sight or lower the front sight.
» To move the point of impact down, lower the rear sight or raise the front sight.
» To move the point of impact right, move the rear sight right or the front sight left.
» To move the point of impact left, move the rear sight left or the front sight right.

Practice goes a long way in making you an accurate and effective handgunner. The most effective means of training is dry-firing, or pulling the trigger with an empty magazine or cylinder. Be careful of simply dry-firing your gun repeatedly. Some striker-fired guns have fragile firing pins and may break after repeated dry-firing. Snap Caps, dummy shells that are made to spec for the most popular handgun rounds, give the firing pin something to hit. Since they're not loaded ammunition, they won't cycle the slide of auto-loaders when a firing pin smacks them.

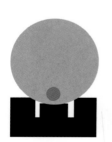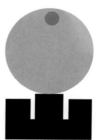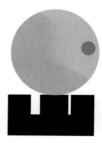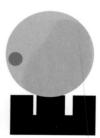

Adjusting your sights to hit on target is a relatively easy proposal; simply follow the shot. If your shots are hitting high, move the front sight up. If they're hitting left, move it that way.

When using notch-and-post sights, align the sight to the base of your target. As you look down the sights of your gun, put the front sight (post) in the rear sight (notch) with equal spacing on both sides, ensuring the three remain level.

Lasers are not new. Albert Einstein first theorized light amplification by stimulated emission of radiation (LASER) in 1917. From 1954 to 1959, Charles Townes and Arthur Schawlow researched and studied the possibility of creating an infrared and visible spectrum light amplification system. In 1960, Theodore Maiman invented the "ruby laser," which was considered the first successful optical or light laser.

If you look through back issues of gun magazines and read about the evolution of high-speed laser sighting systems, you will see the quality and shooter-conscious engineering that goes into visible red and now green laser gun sights has vastly improved.

One type of laser sighting system uses infrared light. To be useful, the shooter must also use some type of night vision optic, as the unaided human eye cannot see infrared light. The infrared laser is beyond the scope of discussion in this topic.

The original designs were, for lack of a better term, ridiculous. Most of these sights hung precariously from trigger guards with wires protruding from them. They might have worked on a sterile test range, but the original laser sights were hardly robust enough for a real-life shooting situation.

Laser lights improve aim and target acquisition, especially indoors.

Modern Laser Sights

Today, visible laser sighting systems, available in either red or green, have become much more commonplace and practical. Regardless of the manufacturer, all laser sights share common characteristics. First, they need a battery source. Second, they require a mounting system to attach the unit securely to a firearm. The actual laser module needs an adjustment mechanism so the end user can zero the laser with the gun bore. Finally, there must be an activation switch or button to turn the unit on and off.

If you examine the numerous offerings from a variety of laser sight makers, you will discover many differences. For instance, Crimson Trace Corp. uses a patented LaserGrip system. The laser sight unit completely replaces the standard factory grip scales on the gun. Other companies, such as LaserMax and LaserLyte, use the original factory screw holes or retaining pins to secure the laser device to the gun frame. Many companies make laser sight units designed for mounting to accessory rails found on the frame of most duty-sized handguns. Others replace the factory recoil spring and guide rod with a laser aiming unit and new spring.

There is wide variance between laser sight manufacturers when it comes to battery life, battery size or battery placement. Since lasers quickly consume battery power, many units include momentary on/off switches. The unit might come with a pressure sensitive pad or button, depending on the make and model. Other characteristics are constant on/off switches or a combination of both.

Inexpensive lasers, a favorite for bargain shoppers, are suited for recreation and not defending your life.

If you choose to install a laser sighting system on your personal defense handgun, ensure the system is robust and ergonomically designed so it's dependable during a violent encounter. Tiny on/off switches that require you to change your grip on the gun are impractical for self-defense applications.

Modern laser lights come with
the on/off switch usually
integrated in the grip.

Laser Sight Misconceptions

Professional instructors share the same opinion of laser sights. The biggest problem with laser sights is the misconceptions that uninformed or inexperienced shooters have about them.

Far too many novice shooters have a misconceived notion that a laser sight guarantees hits on a target. Some people erroneously believe when the laser dot is on the target, when they begin the trigger press, the bullet will hit it. Shooters often believe their laser-sighted pistol excuses them from regular practice. This is simply not the case — it is a myth.

A firearm expert offered this analogy about laser sights, "The laser doesn't press the trigger. Without solid marks-manship fundamentals, the laser is just an expensive toy."

Another misconception is that a laser sight eliminates the need to practice with standard pistol sights. Laser sights are electronic devices. The batteries can die or the circuitry go bad. Laser sights made today are high quality and the power supplies are better than 10 years ago.

Are you willing to bet your life on the laser always working or that you will be able to see it?

In bright daylight, the red dot from a laser sight is difficult, if not impossible, to locate quickly and make a shot. The majority of defensive shootings take place in poor light. Majority does not mean all. You might just need to shoot in good light.

Advanced shooters find the laser sight provides a solid aiming point that facilitates rapid and repeated shot placement.

A laser can provide a reliable source of muzzle direction.

Laser Sight Benefits

Regarding training, particularly for a novice shooter, a laser sight provides an excellent indicator of muzzle direction. The student is reminded that his or her muzzle also covers anything the laser light touches. When practicing follow-up shots, the student can also see the importance of a solid grip for bringing the muzzle back down onto the target.

Advanced shooters find the laser sight provides a solid aiming point that facilitates rapid and repeated shot placement. During emergency shooting situations, the shooter can fire and achieve solid hits even if he or she cannot bring their sights to eye level.

Similarly, gunfights are quick, stressful and often require the shooter to make shots from awkward positions such as shooting from around cover or while moving.

Many shooters who train with a laser-sighted firearm find they are able to achieve solid hits on targets, even in a shooting situation that is less than ideal. The key words in that last sentence are those who train. No sight system eliminates the need to practice or to secure proper training.

Consider poor light shooting situations. Acquiring a practical sight picture in bad light is difficult, even with a luminous Tritium filled front sight. This is where the laser sight truly shines. The red or green laser dot lights up inside buildings and under the heavy shadows of street lamps.

The Viridian C5 is a subcompact weapon mountable green laser.

The Viridian C5L-R is a red laser that fits any railed weapon. Two main advantages include compact size and tight fit.

Red or Green

Many gun owners get confused about choosing between red and green laser sights. People discover both colors are available and wonder which one they should purchase. Here's the difference between them.

The visible red laser sight came first because it was easiest to manufacture in the compact size needed for a handgun unit. Red lasers experienced improvements continuously over several decades. The final product was robust enough to withstand constant recoil and compact enough to be practical. Manufacturers improved red lasers to the point where battery life was reasonable and the power supply minimal.

Visible green lasers were more difficult to put into compact packages for mounting to a firearm. However, the green laser is beginning to catch up with red laser popularity. Green lasers require a larger power supply than the red.

As far as the human eye is concerned, the green laser is most often preferred over the red. The red spectrum is lost or washed out by the sun and is very difficult to pick up beyond a few feet. A brilliant green laser suffers less distortion from sunlight and is more readily perceived by the human eye. Bright green is the last color the eye loses the ability to see when light is diminished; Hence the reason road crews and highway workers wear fluorescent green vests even during daylight.

The Smith & Wesson 637 Airweight .38 Special Revolver comes with this Crimson Trace Laser Grip.

Lasers for Practice and Defense

If you are a child of the '80s, you know Arnold Schwarzenegger first introduced you to the visible red laser on a handgun. When the Terminator walked into a Los Angeles gun shop and asked for a ".45 Longslide with laser sighting" the die was cast. From that moment on, American shooters wanted red lasers on their guns. An interesting piece of trivia younger readers might not be aware of is the origin of that particular movie prop. The laser sight and Longslide M1911 pistol can now be found in the headquarters of SureFire LLC in Fountain Valley, California. Laser Products Corp., the maker of the heretofore-mentioned laser sighting was the precursor to SureFire.

Questionable Practicality

Early laser sight systems were awkward and impractical for use on a handgun. The units were relatively fragile. They would not hold a zero when bumped around. Battery life was limited. Those issues made laser sights rather impractical for genuine fighting work.

Today, visible red and green lasers are practical for daily carry and affordable for the average shooter. Advanced shooters and instructors agree a laser sight on a handgun, rifle or shotgun doesn't negate the need to practice or train.

First Time Out

The following scenario has played out innumerable times at indoor ranges all across the nation. A shooter will purchase his or her first handgun equipped with laser sights, such as the Crimson Trace LaserGrip or Laser-Guard. The shooter steps out onto the range and posts a target at five yards. He or she takes aim with their new laser-equipped handgun while the red dot dances around on the target paper. As the shooter presses the trigger the laser can be seen jerking spasmodically everywhere. Frustrated, the shooter shakes his or her head and comments that there is something wrong with the laser because it won't hold still. In most movies or TV shows the laser dot is rock steady on the target.

Laser sights remain perfectly still when an actor is holding one. This is because they live in the land of make believe. In the real world, where gravity is a factor and the human body is always in motion, lasers on handguns move.

What most neophyte laser shooters don't realize is the movement they can now see via the red or green dot has always been there. They simply never noticed it before.

Using a laser system requires practice, time and training, but doesn't replace the need to practice with iron sights.

Laser Training

The sales pitch for most laser sight devices has normally centered on personal defense. There's nothing wrong with that, although defensive shooting is only part of the equation.

Using a visible laser during live-fire training is an eye-opening experience. But what about using a laser for dry-fire? Many shooters might initially dismiss the idea because nothing is coming out of the muzzle. So, why use a laser?

It is precisely because you can see the movement of the laser dot that makes using them as practice tools so valuable. If the red dot is bouncing all over the landscape by extension, so is the muzzle.

Unfortunately, some people who engage in dry-practice are actually engaging in nothing more than a trigger snapping exercise. Without realizing it, they are ingraining the bad habit of snatching or jerking the trigger. Since no projectile leaves the barrel to mark a target, the shooter doesn't understand the impact of this subtle error.

Incorporate a visible laser into your dry-fire. A shooter can then see how the muzzle moves as he or she applies muscle tension on the handgun while pressing the trigger. Your goal while using the laser is to hold the visible red or green dot as still as humanly possible while pressing the trigger. After a few sessions you will have a good understanding of the value of dedicated dry-fire.

Keep in mind the laser dot will always have some motion. However, that slight movement is of little consequence after you learn to master the trigger press on your gun.

Incorporate a visible laser into your dry-fire. Incorporating a visible laser lets you see how the muzzle moves as you apply muscle tension on the handgun while pressing the trigger.

Benefits are Two-Fold

A handgun equipped with a laser sighting system can have a two-fold benefit. The laser allows you to dry-fire effectively while mastering the trigger press. That skill can be taken to the range to help you get the most of your live-fire practice.

If you're ever forced into a life-threatening situation with the aforementioned pistol, you will now have a carryover skill you can apply. As long as you are willing to put in the time and effort to train and practice, it's a positive situation.

Scary Laser Myth

Regardless of the color, visible lasers benefit and aid the shooter. Laser sights are installed on firearms to direct bullets on target as rapidly and effectively as possible. Shooters should be on guard for the scary laser mythology. Remember, you cannot simply point a laser at people who make you nervous — there is a gun attached to it. As a law-abiding citizen, you can only point a gun at someone who is posing a real and demonstrable threat of death or serious bodily harm. Laser sights on defensive guns are not meant to be toys or a magic talisman. They are serious tools.

Gun mounted laser light systems include specialty products like this Viridian CTL. It clears darkness like a floodlight and stuns attackers with a high-powered strobe.

6: Red Dot Sights

Red dot sights, also known as reflex sights, are gaining popularity among concealed-carry users and home-defense gun owners. Red dot sights are simple to aim and generally improve hit potential under most any condition. Design improvements make battery life longer than ever. The sights are smaller and fit on compact handguns used for self-defense.

Companies like FNH USA and Smith & Wesson offer pistols equipped with red dot sights or manufactured to accept them. Many pistol brands without factory-installed red dots sights accept after-market products using optional mounts.

Training academies and concealed-carry instructors did not always favor red dot sights. They debated that relying on red dot sights diminished the cause for practicing the fundamentals of shooting with iron sights. Red dot sights are gaining credibility in the gun training community as the devices become mainstream with manufacturers. These sights continue to improve with design and remain a common feature on concealed-carry handguns.

Some back-up iron sights are plain, while others have dots or include night sights. All take time to adjust and become accustomed. Some require a change in how the pistol is aimed.

Red Dot Primer

Red dot sights require more training time to effectively master the sights for accuracy and self-defense use. Since an iron-sighted handgun has a short sight radius or distance from the rear to front sight, pistols benefit from the addition of a red dot sight. Most are mounted in front of the rear sight on a combat pistol and closer to the middle on competition pistols. All of the iron sights are removed on a competition pistol. Many shooters may choose to mount red dot sights in-line or above iron sights, depending on the configuration.

Offered in a variety of price ranges, red dot sight prices range from around $100 to several hundred dollars. Dot sizes vary. Some allow for adjustment intensity and a few have power switches. Most stay on all the time or turn off when covered.

The most expensive brands are tested under the harshest conditions. Shooters can adjust all sights for bullet impact, generally with small screwdrivers or other tools. Once adjusted they generally stay that way. Shooters should practice checking their sights while at the range. Back-up iron sights come plain, have dots or include night sights. All of them take time to adjust and get acclimated. Some require a change in how the pistol is aimed.

Red dot sights add another dimension to gun accuracy. Additional training and practice time at the gun range is crucial.

Regularly scheduled battery changes are critical for guns equipped with red dot sights.

Red Dot Battery Life

Practice is imperative with any shooting aid. A red dot sight is no exception. Red dot sights are battery operated and should they fail, the shooter is left without them to rely on for protection. Shooters should engage in regular checking and periodic battery changes. The red dot sight is not a device you use until the battery is completely drained. To determine when a new battery is needed, use the quoted battery life and divide that by four. For example, if the batteries have an expectancy of one year, then you should change them every three months. Battery life quoted in sales literature is the best case scenario and not real world application.

Red Dot Design

Pistols used for law enforcement, military duty or self-protection must have iron sights. They may be secondary if the pistol uses a red dot. Iron sights are a must for back-up use.

Red dot sights come in two basic designs. Smith & Wesson and FNH USA mount the red dot in front of the rear sight. This allows you to sight through the red dot using the iron sights. Lone Wolf Distributors and other companies make slides for Glock pistols designed to use these sights. They also mount the red dot at the rear of the slide with the rear iron sight in front. Most 1911 pistols designed for self-defense have the mount just forward of the rear sight. All require taller iron sights originally designed for use with a suppressor.

Revolvers are different since dovetailing a sight into the top strap proves problematic if even possible at all. Most use a rail that attaches to the top strap with the sight mounted on top of it.

Pistols with iron sights in front or behind the red dot come down to personal preference. Both methods work equally well in most conditions. Theoretically, the closest sight to your eye is the primary sight. In practice it seems to matter little.

Some shooters like the rear sight behind the red dot sight. Longtime shooters favor such configurations because their eyes are trained to look for the front sight and ignore the rear sight unless needed. It also allows shooters to use pistols with no red dot without altering an established aiming pattern. Looking for the dot and ignoring the front sight takes practice for experienced pistol shooters. It is not uncommon for competitive shooters to remove the iron sights.

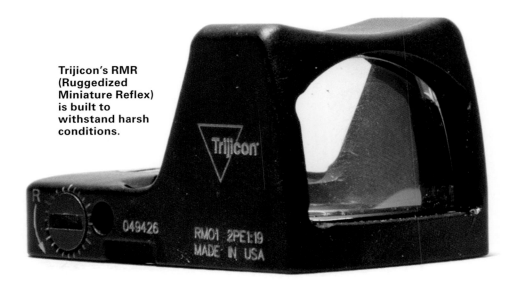

Trijicon's RMR (Ruggedized Miniature Reflex) is built to withstand harsh conditions.

Red Dot Sight Options

Several companies offer proven red dot sights suitable for pistols. Leupold's Delta-Point offers a 3.5 MOA (Minute of Angle) dot and a 7.5 MOA triangle. A dot sight at 3.5 MOA measures approximately 3.5 inches at 100 yards, meaning it will completely cover 3.5 inches of target at that range. At 50 yards, a 3.5 MOA dot covers 1.75 inches and 0.875 inches at 25 yards. Given pistol ranges are most often 25 yards or less, the triangle allows for some precision using the tip of the triangle for precise aiming and the body for fast shots.

Trijicon's RMR (Ruggedized Miniature Reflex) is another popular sight. It is built to withstand harsh conditions. It is available with fixed and adjustable LED in both a 3.25 and 6.5 MOA dot. Trijicon also offers a dual illumination model with fiber optics and tritium, removing the need for batteries. It is offered with a dot or triangle in green or amber. The smallest dot is 7.0 MOA with models as large as 13.0 MOA available.

A relative newcomer to the game is Vortex and the Razor reflex sight. This rugged and reliable model is offered in either a 3.0 or 6.0 MOA dot. A side access battery compartment makes battery changes easy and offers the ability to adjust intensity. The ability to power off when not in use also contributes to longer battery life.

Another excellent micro-dot is Leupold's MRDS (Mini Red Dot Sight). It has a 3.5 or 7 MOA dot that can be adjusted manually or automatically. It is also night vision capable. The top loading battery compartment makes changes easy and it can be turned off for storage.

The Burris FastFire is considered by many as the most popular red dot sight. It is proving to be very reliable at less than half the cost of the top tier units. The FastFire II uses a 4 MOA dot. Their latest model, the FastFire III, is available with a 3 or 8 MOA dot. This model allows for battery changes without removing the sight, adjustments without tools and brightness settings with a low battery indicator.

There are also less expensive sights, although most do not hold up under recoil and should not be used on a carry pistol.

The FNX-45 with a
mounted laser red dot
sight.

Leupold's DeltaPoint offers
a 3.5 MOA (Minute of
Angle) dot and a 7.5 MOA
triangle.

Holsters for Red Dot Sights

Choosing a holster with red dot sights requires trial and research to find a fit for your gun. Many standard holsters do not accept guns with large iron sights or even red dot adapted versions, however the industry is catching up. Several companies offer concealed carry holsters to accommodate these pistols.

Blade-Tech and Blackhawk are two large holster and gun accessory manufacturers that accommodate red dot sights. Some makers offer products that will even carry pistols with red dot sights for IWB (Inside Waistband) holsters. Several companies make custom holsters as well, providing an ever growing option for shooters to carry red dot equipped pistols for concealed carry.

Red Dot Practice

Making the addition of red dot sights to your gun arsenal requires additional practice time. That is especially true with drawing the gun from a holster used for concealed-carry use. For years, pistol makers have rounded off corners and otherwise melted their pistols for concealed carry. Even so, the reduced size still does not provide total concealment for a handgun. A gun equipped with a red dot sight and a front sight can snag on clothing or other items when drawn from a holster for use.

Be certain you can safely remove your pistol without snagging on clothing and return it safely to the holster. Carrying and concealing a gun with red dot sights may require a wardrobe change but it is all part of carrying a concealed firearm. Shooters should identify issues during dry-fire or on the range, not on the street.

Along with checking for concealment issues make certain to run significant amounts of ammunition through your red dot equipped pistol to make sure it works. Pistols with slides can be very sensitive to the weight of a red dot sight. How quickly the slide goes to the rear and returns to battery can affect the overall timing of the pistol. Slowing it down or speeding it up too much can cause serious malfunctions, especially with 1911 pistols. The slide may require a different return spring with some pistols.

Be certain to to fire both your practice ammunition as well as your self-defense rounds through your gun — they are almost always different. Just because your gun runs smoothly with FMJ does not mean it will run self-defense ammunition. More powerful ammunition also influences slide speed, adding to the entire equation.

Malfunction drills and reloads may require a change, depending on the pistol. Rolling over the top to rack the slide means you are going to run into that sight. Small hands may have more issues. Running the gun hard may stress the sight. If there are buttons, make sure that your chosen technique does not turn off the sight. Some pistol manufacturers do not recommend using the slide stop to release the slide. You must run the gun through everything normally with the gear you typically use to verify that it all works.

Red dot laser sights require additional practice to become familiar with their operation.

Caught in the Dark

Confidence gained during the beginner stage of handgun use encourages the search for more discoveries. These findings go beyond what you encounter during a weekend at the gun range. This is especially the case if your handgun interest goes beyond protecting the lives of yourself and loved ones.

The world is an imperfect place and crime awaits everywhere, even in the dark.

Most of us understand that violent crime and assaults occur predominantly during the hours of darkness or in diminished light situations. Each year, FBI statistics show police officers are attacked and killed up to 70 percent of the time during hours of darkness or diminished light.

The cruel irony of that situation is the vast majority of firearm training is conducted when the light is the best, not the worst. Shooting ranges close during foul weather and darkness. Most outdoor public and private ranges have strict rules about shooting after sunset.

Trying to find a place where you can practice in the dark is difficult. If you are serious about defending your life with a concealed-carry handgun, try to seek out realistic training alternatives or find a gun school or training academy that prepares you for shooting in low light conditions.

Light Vision

Consider the following scenario. It is 2 a.m. and you are awakened from bed in a panic. Your dog is furiously barking when you hear a crashing sound. Your adrenaline begins racing as you grab a pistol and flashlight from the nightstand. You have children asleep in their bedrooms and their safety is at the forefront of your mind.

For the above scenario ask yourself the following question. Will I be able to effectively aim and defend my family in total darkness? "No" is the likely answer. When a person is startled from sleep, he or she is most likely unprepared and could do more harm than good in the dark.

Here's another thought-provoking question, especially if you regularly wear prescription glasses. Will I remember to put my glasses on so I can see? The answer is up to you, but consider the consequences should you not wear them. Even so, what if they are knocked off in a struggle with an intruder?

Our eyes require more light to function normally as we age. It is a simple fact of growing older. The eyes of someone over the age of 40 require more light to see clearly than those of a 20-year-old person. Older eyes require three to four times more light to function as they did when younger. As we age, vision issues include reduced ability to see contrast, colors and impaired depth perception. There is also an increase in the amount of time it takes for the eyes to transition from light to dark or vice versa.

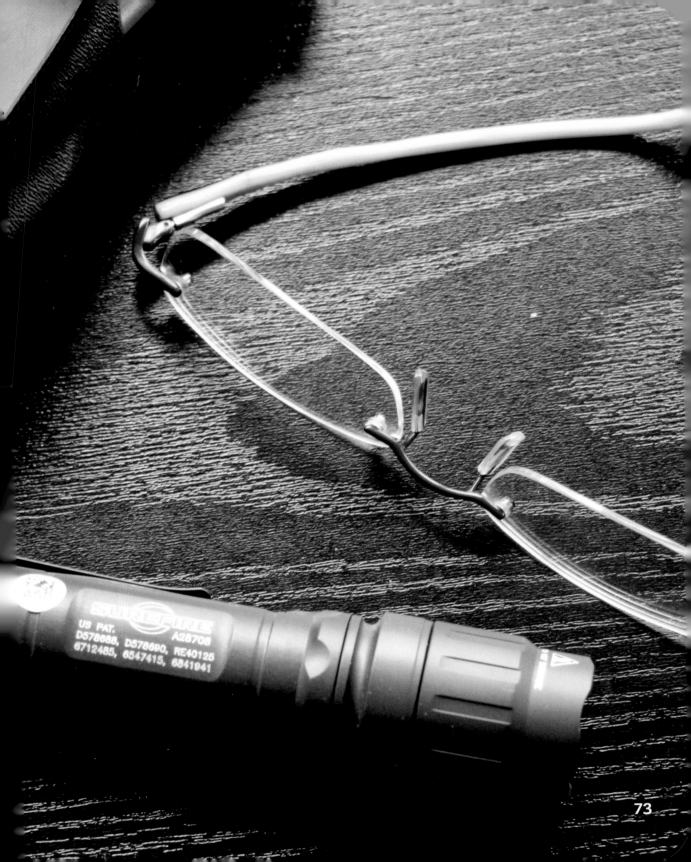

Training in the Dark

Operating a handgun while using a handheld light is another skill that must be learned and practiced. You can practice the techniques in the daylight on your average shooting range. However, the culmination of your learning should take place in actual darkness on a live-fire range. The best place to learn such skills is at an academy or training school that conducts training after dark.

There are several professional firearms schools such as Gunsite Academy in Prescott, Arizona, that offer advanced fighting courses where students engage targets in the dark. Gunsite Academy allows students to train indoors, in urban scenarios. Some students use brands such as the SureFire flashlight to clear rooms. In specially designed buildings, shooters can practice with shoot and no-shoot full-color targets.

If you have only practiced slow-fire shooting on a square range in ample light, clearing a building in the dark with a flashlight is quite an eye opening experience. Any person who is serious about protecting their loved ones with firearms should aspire to this type of training.

A rugged flashlight with LED lights is essential gear for concealed carry use in the dark.

White Light

More light is always better than less. The best tool available to help you make up for aging vision deficiencies is white light in the form of artificial light. Tactical or combat lights should all share certain characteristics, regardless of the deployment system. All handheld lights should have a solid, focused beam of unbroken light. Cheap flashlights have dead spots due to poorly constructed reflectors.

White LED lights provide many benefits. With an LED light, there are no bulb filaments to break. LED lights offer tremendous battery-life and run time. However, beware of the cheap Chinese LED lights. They are worthless for anything beyond finding keys in the dark.

Light strength is measured in lumens. Lumens measure the entire output of the light beam. Candlepower measures the brightest spot of the light. In general, 60 to 100 Lumen lights are good for utility. Newer lights in the 200 to 400 Lumen range provide more than enough light for fighting. A light that is small enough to be carried in a pocket and 100 plus lumens should get you through the night.

For handheld tactical lights, the switch should be some form of push button at the base of the light. The push button allows you to find the light easily in complete darkness with either hand. It is crucial that the light is sturdy and robust. Cheap lights will break; high quality lights will not.

Flashlight Techniques

Numerous schools of thought exist of how to employ a handheld light in conjunction with a handgun. One technique includes FBI instruction. The shooter holds the flashlight far away from the body with a support hand to hide his or her actual position to confuse an attacker. This technique works for hasty situations. It is difficult to use for extended periods due to arm fatigue.

There is now a new Modified FBI technique. As the shooter moves the support hand and searches with the light, the handgun is controlled near the body with the strong hand. This technique works well for room clearing.

The Harries flashlight technique is another useful method. With this technique, the shooting hand rests on the top of the flashlight hand and crossed in back-to-back fashion. This grip offers a much greater amount of stability and is a good way to engage a target. However, the method works very poorly for building clearing.

Some shooters favor the Cigar or Syringe technique. With this method, the handheld light is pinched between the forefinger and middle finger of the support hand. Pressing the tail cap switch with the palm activates the light. The Cigar technique allows the shooter to put both hands together and offers more support. This method is decent for shooting but poor for searching.

Another method called the Neck Index technique is an instinctive and natural way for most students to employ both a handheld light and handgun together. With this method, the the flashlight is held in an overhand grip with the support hand and searches in the Original FBI method. If a shooter must engage in shooting, the flashlight is brought back quickly to his or her body and indexed along the neck and collarbone area. The shooter then firmly grips the pistol with his or her strong hand and prepares to shoot.

A shooter practices the Modified FBI technique on the live-fire range.

The Neck Index method is used for rapid target engagement, not for searching.

Light Primer

Facing a deadly attack in the dark is a terrifying proposition. Unfortunately an assault in the dark or under poor light conditions is statistically very likely. We cannot expect that bad people will have the common courtesy to only attack us on sunny Sunday afternoons.

The first step in dealing with the reality of an attack in the dark is to accept that it can happen. Steps two and three include arming yourself with the best training and equipment available. Tools without training are merely toys. When a shooter combines the two steps, he or she will obtain the skills and genuine confidence if a bad situation occurs.

Early on, many handgun carriers also carried a flashlight with them and not only for lighting up the darkness. The additional light helped handgun carriers to aid and identify potential problems, even in daylight. The flashlight allowed the shooter to see and confirm that a threat really existed and to react accordingly.

As flashlights became more powerful, they emerged as useful weapons for projecting blinding levels of light. Entire low light training doctrines and schools developed. The training program focused on the use of light. Eventually, stronger lights became required equipment for concealed carry use.

At the same time, weapon mounted lights gained popularity on tactical teams. Earlier versions were large, heavy and low power and mounting was a nightmare. However, over the years, gun-mounted lights experienced many improvements as they became smaller, increasingly powerful and more reliable. Attaching rails to the bottom of the pistol made installation simple and effective. As they gained popularity, long gun manufacturers began building their pistols with light rails integrated into the lower receiver. Pistol mounted lights soon became mandatory equipment for tactical teams.

Gun-mounted lights remain a popular, standard option for many shooters. As lights became more reliable and easier to use, they migrated into the law enforcement patrol sector. Having a light on a pistol greatly benefits officers. Kydex duty holsters that easily accepted pistols with lights became affordable. Initially these were only seen in duty holsters, however non-law enforcement began carrying them as well. As the holster industry evolved, companies designed concealed carry holsters to accept a light, while remaining comfortable, concealable and usable. Lights today are more affordable, longer lasting and more user friendly.

Pistol-mounted lights are popular for law enforcement use. They are equally as functional for personal protection.

79

Some shooters install pistol-mounted lights as accessories to their handguns.

Pistol Mount Light Uses

Pistol mounted light use requires training and a clear understanding of their purpose. The primary function of any weapon-mounted light should include navigation and threat identification. Some shooters mount pistol-mounted lights as accessories to their handguns. A pistol-mounted light is ideal if the situation requires locating someone posing a deadly threat. You can navigate through the prevailing environment while searching for deadly threats safely and confidently. While maintaining a proper grip, the threat can be identified. The lights improve accuracy, provide better recoil control and maneuverability and bring your front sight to the eye even without night sights to increase accuracy. Pistol-mounted lights remain the best tool for searching and identifying deadly threats in low or failing light.

Shooters can also use pistol-mounted lights as a weapon. They emit blinding light that can disorient a threat and possibly negate the need for deadly force. Powerful pistol lights can distract threats long enough to take alternate action. The latest pistol lights emit light levels that may produce pain at close range and disorient a person. Many provide strobes that add to this effect.

The SureFire X300 is a popular choice for a pistol-mounted light.

Pistol Mount Lights and Flashlights

Many law enforcement officials prefer a dedicated secondary handheld flashlight. Shooters can use weapon-mounted lights as an aggressive tool if needed. The best defense against bright light is one that is brighter. These lights are available to anyone. If you are confronted by an attacker with a bright light, combat it by directing your light at his or her light.

Shooters should never use weapon-mounted lights as a general searching tool. Weapon-mounted lights are not a tool used to search for evidence, or the best way to access the refrigerator at night. A light mounted to your weapon should never be your only light source. If there is no need for a pistol, there is no need for a pistol light.

Shooters should carry at least one other handheld light for general searching, reading or navigation where no threat of deadly force exists. Many use rechargeable handheld lights for general searching and as a primary light. Smaller lithium powered lights remain accessible all the time and are beneficial for general use. Shooters who choose to carry a weapon-mounted light for concealed carry or self-protection should follow a similar protocol. Your pistol light should never act as a substitute for a well-made handheld light that fits comfortably on your person.

Using a handheld and pistol-mount light is a popular and effective tactic.

Light Functions

Various weapon light systems provide several means for activation. Most have a button switch at the rear of the light. Some are momentary, meaning they stay on as long as you hold the switch. Other systems operate in either constant on or off mode. Some systems use this same switch to activate a strobe effect, while others may have a true off switch that disables the light. How you choose to use these switches depends on the weapon, available light and your hand. Shooters who grip the pistol with their thumbs forward can activate a light switch with their off hand thumb. This leaves the control hand free to manipulate the trigger as needed. You can also use your trigger finger. However, when this method is used with a momentary switch, it will turn the light off as you move to the trigger.

Some shooters prefer remote switches for pistol-mounted lights. Many provide a replacement cap that provides a remote switch for mounting on the side of the pistol. Most are better suited for long guns, although they can work on a pistol. Some users attach the switch to the grip while others attach them to the side of the lower frame.

On some pistols the light can be activated from the grip.

83

Training and Use

When using these methods shooters should spend considerable dry-fire time operating the light to make sure it works properly when searching. A productive way to train on light use is to purchase a facsimile pistol. Several companies make precise copies of common pistols for attaching a light. This allows you to work around the house without the danger of an accident with your pistol. It is also crucial to practice on a live fire range. Holding your light on target while searching is easy, however the recoil can move the light off target.

One should exercise care when using gun-mounted lights in a holster. The light can also hook on items during the draw. Newer designs provide switches that mold to the trigger guard of the pistols. This method is quickly becoming a favorite of many shooters as it allows a person to operate the light and pistol with one hand. Your standard grip is maintained throughout the entire searching process. A shooter can easily activate the light and not worry about it falling off when firing. A standard two-hand grip is maintained. Most gun-mounted lights interfere little if at all with specialized holsters. A shooter can use a secondary light in conjunction with the weapon's light if necessary. Depending on how you grip the pistol it will activate every time you acquire the grip.

A shooter can operate the light with his or her trigger finger. However, this method when used with a momentary switch, will turn the light off as you move to the trigger.

Light Effects

It is important to recognize the use of any light has at least two effects. The first is assisting in search and navigation. The other is revealing a threat in your immediate environment.

During training and practice time, it is important to exercise control when using lights. Shooters should avoid unintentional activation of the light if at all possible. Momentary activation is crucial. If you don't need the light to see where you are going or identify a possible threat, then leave it off. Bright and powerful white light disables night vision.

Powerful lights illuminate a large area. Always avoid backlighting someone else who is with you. When light is shined behind something it silhouettes anyone that is in front. It provides a perfect target for any threat for which you are searching. When behind or beside someone, it is critical to be discriminating about light use. When the threat shows itself, you will likely point your light and your pistol in that direction. Even if it does not result in you pointing your pistol directly at your partner, it may light them up from behind. Light reflects off any flat surface. The more reflective the surface and the closer you are, the more the light reflects.

It's easy to forget a light extends in an ever larger, yet less powerful cone. Always be aware of where the light shines.

Light Power

In low light conditions, it is difficult to tell the depth of a room. Depth perception is reduced. Turning on a light in a confined space could blind you temporarily. Pistol lights are not suited for small rooms. As handy as these lights are, they do not substitute for handheld lights and their appropriate use. You need to train on both and learn how to use them separately and together. Shooters should use their secondary light and search with it only using the pistol light if necessary.

Powerful lights have a center section that is obvious to you when behind them. It's easy to forget the light extends in an ever larger, yet less powerful cone. The light is less powerful yet completely visible at the edges of this cir-

cle. The edge of the light will extend to ceilings and floors, and can even make you visible through doors and windows. It's important to stay alert and aware of where the light shines. Do not get locked into the center of the light.

It is critical that your pistol light is only on when it's directed at a perceived threat. The powerful light should allow you to see and aim more efficiently and at the same time temporarily blind the threat.

Weapon-mounted lights remain controversial with concealed-carry and handgun instructors. When used improperly or inappropriately, the lights can be a liability. When used properly and under the correct circumstances, pistol-mounted lights are effective tools.

9: Holsters & Their Use

"Carrying a gun is supposed to be comforting, not comfortable" is an adage the gun-toting community spouts when questions arise about comfort while carrying. While the saying might be true in many cases, when outfitted with a reasonable gun and quality holster, carrying a gun can be comfortable as well.

With concealed carry options, tradeoffs abound. You can have a full-size big-bore autoloader, but some permit holders find it a challenge to pack it comfortably and discreetly. On the flip side, a small snubnose .38 Special or .380 ACP both pack nicely into your pocket or purse, but they don't offer the firepower of the larger guns. Consequently, finding a gun you're comfortable with is of the utmost impor-

tance. You must then decide where you're going to pack your gun. Once you determine this, the potentially mind-boggling search for a holster begins.

Classic leather pieces offer light weight and class, but Kydex has eaten up much of the leather market with its typically lower price, durability and versatility. Regardless of the material you choose, you'll likely be most satisfied if you opt for a holster made for your particular gun and desired carry position. Tailor-made rigs make for a more comfortable fit and carry experience. After all, if your gun isn't comfortable to carry, you are more likely to leave it at home. If you're familiar with Mr. Murphy and his infamous law, it'll be on the dresser when it needs to be in your hand.

» Civilian Holsters

Concerning guns, money or any other necessity, it's better to have and not need than to need and not have. This is the defining rule of why people choose to carry a concealed handgun. If you were going someplace and knew you would need a gun, you'd be wise to simply stay home. If knowing when you'd need a gun was an option, there'd be no need to carry one. You would simply avoid those situations. Since we live in the real world and you never know when you might to need a gun, it's best to have one on hand.

The two main issues with carrying a gun full-time are ease of concealment and comfort while carrying. These questions weigh heavy in the process of selecting which gun is best for you as well as the manner in which you'll carry it. Even if you decide to carry in your pocket or purse, use a holster to keep the gun in a position where it is easily drawn and to cover the trigger.

Without a holster protecting the trigger, your gun jostles loose in your purse or pocket and in a worst-case scenario, your jeans may grab on a drawer handle and contact the trigger. Now you've got a hole in your floor and possibly your leg.

Now that you know you need a holster for your gun, where do you want to carry it?

Holster Materials

Leather

As previously mentioned, leather used to be the only serious option for carrying a gun, concealed or not. Leather remains a viable option when done correctly. Many generic pistol holsters come up short in terms of properly hiding your gun. Avoid holsters that are not made specifically for your gun. Generic holsters typically don't keep tension on your gun or have retaining straps, which could mean your gun squeezes out of the holster during everyday activities, such as sitting.

Only consider holsters that are tailor-made for your gun. They keep pressure on the weapon in all the right places and don't have any extra material that adds unnecessary bulk to your rig.

Leather holsters, like boots, often become more comfortable with age and use. A "break-in" period will make the leather more supple and loosen the vice-like grip some give at first. Practicing your draw and re-holstering will properly break in a leather holster. These can also be some of the most elegant and refined holsters you'll ever see.

One of the drawbacks of leather is the price — sometimes. Those with a high price tag are often highly sought after and may have a lengthy backorder from smaller manufacturers. However, if they're pricey and in demand, that's probably because they're quality holsters. This material may also get hot, as leather riding against your skin all day will make that part of your hip sweat, even on cold days. Imagine wearing boots without socks. The salt in your sweat can damage the finish of the holster and even rust the gun. However, an undershirt remedies these issues. Leather holsters often feature leather loops or plastic hooks to affix the rig to your belt. Both are viable options.

Kydex

The most popular material favored by today's pistol packers is Kydex, a hard plastic material. It has high rigidity and is thin for how strong it is, meaning Kydex holsters are often less bulky and stronger than comparable leather ones. Law enforcement and tactical operators now prefer custom Kydex holsters because of their lightweight and versatility. Even custom Kydex holsters, like those made by Birmingham, Alabama based Rule of Concealment (www.ruleofconcealment.com) are affordable and available in a host of options from retention style, degree of cant (tilt) and color, ensuring your holster fits both you and your gun.

Kydex is a strong, lightweight plastic that is easily molded to fit any handgun. This outside-the-waistband holster, from Rule of Concealment (www.ruleofconcealment.com) is made just for a Smith & Wesson M&P .45 with a rail-mounted light.

According to Ryan Gale, owner and sole employee of Rule of Concealment, the only drawback of Kydex is a small one. "It can scratch your gun if it gets dirty where it contacts the gun," he says.

Regardless of the material or position of your holster, make sure you're comfortable with it. You're far more likely to carry your gun if it's easy and comfortable to carry.

Carry Options

A finite number of places exist where you can carry your gun that keeps it both concealed and accessible. Deep concealment, such as appendix carry (in front on your belt) may work for summer when light clothes may be the order of the day, but the further stashed away your gun is, the harder it is to retrieve. This especially rings true when you're under stress. For example, an ankle holster is about as concealed as it gets, but a gun on your ankle is also the most difficult to retrieve. A gun on your hip is the easiest to retrieve but it's also the most obvious place to pack a pistol. Tradeoffs aside, a gun placed along your waistline remains the most popular option due to the natural placement and easy concealment. However, some carry permit holders prefer other options.

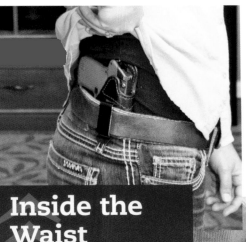

Many of those who carry concealed weapons prefer inside the waistband holsters. Ideally these holsters hook onto a belt and allow a gun to sit inside the pants against one's hip. Because the gun stays inside the belt loop, they are often more comfortable and easier to conceal.

Outside the Waist

Another popular method, outside-the-waistband or OWB places the muzzle of the gun on the outside of your pants. You won't need new pants with this method, but the gun is slightly less concealed. Permit holders prefer this method in the colder months when they wear a jacket or coat.

Inside the Waist

Inside-the-waistband carrying, often referred to as IWB, is the most common way of carrying a concealed pistol. It's popular with both large and small guns as well as people of all sizes, but a trim waistline makes this method more comfortable. Permit holders typically carry IWB between the three o'clock and four o'clock position. Though popular, IWB carry adds at least an inch to your waistline since the barrel or slide of the gun rides inside your pants.

Carrying your gun outside of your waistband requires a higher degree of concealment, as it's more exposed. This is also the most comfortable way to carry a gun, and is very easy to draw.

Pocket

As the name implies, this method simply involves you sliding your gun (often a small auto-loader or revolver) into your pocket. Though your pocket works as a holster of sorts, you still need a specific pocket holster to both cover the trigger and keep the gun in proper orientation for a speedy draw. Desantis offers several models to fit popular handguns.

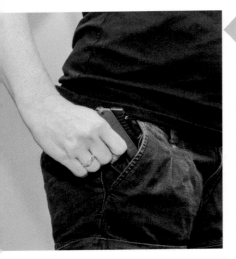

For deep concealment, pocket carry is hard to beat. The downside is that the draw isn't the fastest. A holster is a must when choosing pocket carry.

Appendix carry is not for everyone. The draw is fast, but sitting can be uncomfortable with larger guns. Those with a slim frame can carry this way better.

Off-body carry is a popular choice among women; you're already carrying a purse, so you might as well make it your pistol toter, too.

Appendix

This method is similar to IWB, but the gun rides at roughly the one o'clock position, if noon were your belt buckle. Drawbacks to appendix carry include an uncomfortable position when sitting. This carry method usually requires a slim figure.

Off-body Carry

Carrying off your body is a double-edged sword; it's the most comfortable way to carry a gun, but can also be the most worrisome. Suppose you leave your purse in a restaurant, or it gets snatched in a crowd somewhere. Though extremely undesired in the fashion world, a fanny pack provides the best and most practical choice for off-body carry. Several manufacturers make fanny packs just for carry.

If you opt to carry in your purse, you'll still need a holster, unless you get a purpose-built purse. Galco and several other well-known holster makers make "gun purses" that look no different on the outside from any other leather purse. These keep your gun separate from the rest of the purse's contents, keeping you from pawing it unnecessarily.

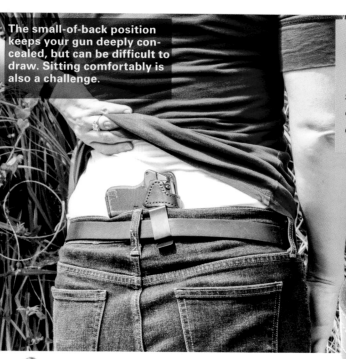

The small-of-back position keeps your gun deeply concealed, but can be difficult to draw. Sitting comfortably is also a challenge.

Small of the Back

Carrying a gun here is easy, but drawing is slow since you have to reach clear to the middle of your back to procure the weapon. Sitting comfortably can also prove challenging.

A good, thick belt is a must when choosing to carry a gun around your waist. Thin belts will sag and not properly support the gun. Look for a belt with a width of at least 1 1/2 inch.

Ankle and Shoulder

These methods are worth mentioning, but are rarely used by serious pistol packers. A gun stuck to your ankle is almost impossible to retrieve in a smooth and timely manner without contorting and bending over. Shoulder holsters are cumbersome and require extra garments to conceal. However, shoulder holsters allow you to conceal bigger guns and spare magazines very easily.

The Belt

If you choose to wear your pistol on your person, either on your belt or in your pocket, you've got to wear a good belt. If you've got a 1-pound gun and hang it off of a 1/2-inch-wide belt, the gun won't stay put for long. It'll droop and weigh you down. While maybe not the most fashionable, a belt in the 1 1/2- to 1 3/4-inch range works much better when carrying a gun. Even a small pistol in your pocket warrants a thick, good-fitting belt.

93

» Law Enforcement Holsters

Choosing the appropriate holster is always critical. It is even more so for law enforcement. Duty holsters expose pistols to the elements, environment and criminals. Law Enforcement professionals must often run towards the gunfire, so a working pistol is crucial in a dangerous situation.

Duty holsters must carry and secure the pistol during vigorous activity to include running, climbing, crawling on the ground or fighting with a suspect. At the same time, they must allow a fast and secure draw that is achievable under stress. The holsters must accomplish these tasks while protecting the pistol from damage while professionals carry it for long hours.

Ultimately, shooters must strike a compromise between retention and the ability to draw quickly. A number of factors come into play, which include skill level and willingness to practice. Other factors include budget and the environment in which the gun and holster must perform.

Duty holsters must allow a fast and secure draw that is achievable under stress.

94

Retention and Access

Retention is important for a holster in this category. Defined, retention is how secure the holster retains the pistol. Realistically, that equates to the number of straps or devices on the holster that the shooter must disengage to remove the pistol.

Access is equally as important. Access determines how easily the officer, under stress, can draw the pistol. Greater retention lessens accessibility. Conversely, less retention equates to more accessibility.

Duty holsters range from single to triple or even more retention. Single retention holsters have one means of retention. It can be a strap, button or the amount of tension placed on the gun while in the holster. Single retention holsters provide the least security and the fastest or least complicated draw.

Dual retention holsters have tension coupled with a second means of security. These holsters may include rotating hoods, buttons, straps or even a need to twist the pistol prior to removing it.

Triple retention holsters add a third strap or device. They provide the most security, while requiring significant practice specifically if officers must draw under stress.

Minimal retention holds the pistol in the holster under rigorous activity. Further retention makes it harder for someone other than the officer to remove the gun. Either factor can be lethal to an officer. Having a pistol fall out is never good. Getting it taken away is worse. However, being unable to draw it from the holster is equally as lethal. The holster needs to strike the balance that best suits your needs and the conditions under which you work.

Most retention devices consist of hoods, buttons or similar mechanical devices. Some use straps. Simulated leather and basket weave finishes make these holsters practical for most uniformed assignments. The similarity of these holsters and their configurations also allow an officer to use a tactical holster that is identical to their duty holster. Durable polymer holsters are incredibly strong and very rigid. That makes them well suited to outside carry for long hours.

Single retention holsters provide the least security and the fastest or least complicated draw.

Holster Materials

Policy often dictates holster construction. Holster makers typically use one of three materials: leather, Nylon or plastic (Kydex or other polymers). They may also use of a combination of those materials.

Leather remains the primary choice for wearing with dress uniforms and for units in constant public view. The manufacturing process makes tight molding to the pistol more difficult. Retention is less pronounced, making dual retention the minimum for any exposed uniform position. Leather holsters are practical when using a thumb snap or strap. Leather is tough, durable and lends itself to polishing, although that can be costly. Leather holsters also require a break-in period.

Holsters built from polymers are fast becoming the choice of law enforcement officials. The holsters mold around the pistol, including tactical lights. A break-in period is unnecessary and these holsters hold up well under harsh conditions. Most are impervious to oils, chemicals or the elements. Holsters made of polymers remain durable and lasting for years of use. Tight molding promotes more tension.

Nylon holsters are still available but are becoming rare. Kydex and other polymer materials are becoming more practical for holster design, manufacture and use. Well-made nylon can be very strong, lightweight and rugged. Molding is rare unless combined with Kydex. Only the highest quality Nylon holsters are stiff enough to provide adequate protection and retention. Some tactical units still utilize these Nylon holsters.

Nylon holsters can remain thin and are very quiet during movement. Nylon is usually the least expensive alternative. Nylon is better suited to wet environments where the pistol is completely covered. Nylon remains the best choice for tactical units and law enforcement personnel that must match the holster to camouflage.

The latest varieties of duty holsters combine more than one of these materials. Some use Kydex internally with leather on the outside. Kydex holsters with Nylon exteriors are also gaining some popularity. They provide solid retention yet add the more stealthy properties of Nylon.

Those who wear uniforms still mostly prefer leather holsters.

97

Holster Selection

You should always base holster selection on a mix of retention and access. The most popular choice remains the holster with the least amount of retention necessary for the environment, while allowing for the greatest access to the draw.

Officers are more likely to be injured or killed due to a failure to access their pistol rather than retaining it from an attack. Weapons retention involves several factors. Proven officer safety practices and training can mitigate the need for excessive retention devices. However, when you must draw your weapon, you generally have no second chance. Failing to access your weapon because you could not defeat retention devices under stress will get you killed.

If at all possible, use the same means of retention all the time. If you have a separate tactical holster, make it the same style as your uniformed duty holster. Choose holsters with exactly the same retention devices. Even plain-clothes duty holsters allow this match. You want to pattern and practice only one means of removing the pistol under stress and otherwise.

Never field a new holster without significant dry-fire practice. Practice with a new holster on your hip as the feeling is different than pulling the pistol from the holster off the hip. Dry practice so that you know you can properly use the weapon and holster.

Accessing the pistol under stress is all about training and practice. Never assume your new holster works. Even the best companies have errors in production. Surviving to retirement as an officer involves awareness, preparation, training and practice.

You may never even use your pistol. If you do, the time will be short. Mistakes will be compounded and failures to prepare or train lethal. Take the time to choose the best possible duty holster. Be certain you can use it properly under stress. It just may save the life of you or someone else.

Always base holster selection on a mix of retention and access.

» Combat Holsters

Combat holsters are an integral part of the combat dress uniform.

A holster, by definition is merely a device used to secure your handgun when not in use. The modern holster manufacturing industry is a million dollar enterprise that provides a huge variety of handgun holsters to the worldwide market. They provide such a plethora of products and variety of designs that the consumer can become lost in a sea of leather, plastic and Kydex. Combat holsters are no exception when it comes to variety.

A combat or fighting holster must provide a robust and durable platform. Fighting holsters must hold the gun securely in place regardless of the weather or environmental conditions. The pistol must stay secure whether or not the operator is getting in or out from vehicles or running across the ground. However, the holster unit still needs to be lightweight and practical. No one would wear a two-pound holster, no matter how tough it is.

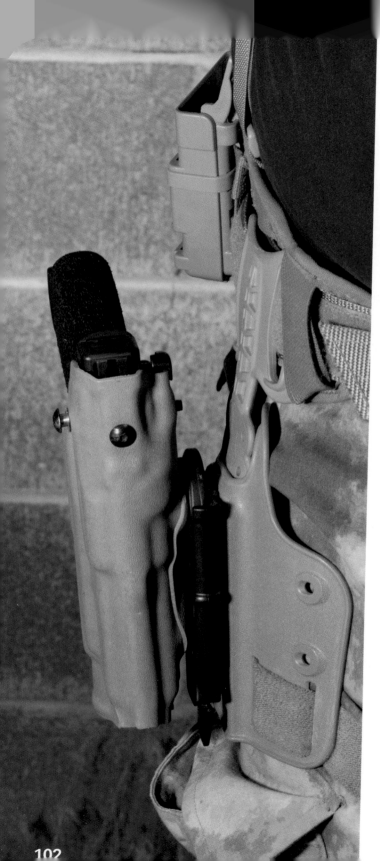

Retention Systems

Every combat holster must have some type of retention system to secure the gun in place. Some of the greatest diversity amongst manufacturers takes place in this area. Opinions vary with different types of retention systems and, more specifically, how users operate the retention systems.

For decades, holster makers have been attempting to outdo each other with different retention systems. In the modern world of holsters, professionals describe retention as passive and active. A passive retention system activates as soon as the user puts the gun into the holster. No other actions on the part of the shooter are necessary. The Blackhawk SERPA holster presents a good example of a holster with a passive retention system.

An active retention system requires the user to activate some type of strap, snap, buckle, hood or other securing device. The classic active retention system is the thumb-break snap. The most popular fighting holster with an active retention system is likely the Safariland Model 6004.

Having seen the merits of both retention systems, most major manufacturers of combat holsters have been working on hybrid versions that employ both a passive and active retention system. Blackhawk's EPOCH holster is a good example, as well as the brand's SERPA Level III Duty Holster. This unit has both the passive SERPA lock and an active security hood.

Safariland modified their existing Model 6004 holster with their new Self-Locking System (SLS). It's combined with an original active rotating hood. Both the Safariland and Blackhawk holsters provide ample retention and are robust enough for the United States military.

Ergonomics

Over the years, there have been a number of improvements made to holsters, claiming to be the most secure holster on the market. The trouble with security is that at some point in time, the end user is going to need to get their gun out. When a good guy needs his pistol, he needs it quickly. Cumbersome snaps, straps and buckles that are difficult to operate under stress are a bad idea.

As a rule, the shooter should be able to access his pistol, draw it and fire a shot on target in a maximum time of two seconds. Shooters will find this task difficult if the holster doesn't have proper ergonomics. A good combat holster retention system operates with the natural movements of the shooters hands, not against them.

As a rule, the shooter should be able to access his pistol, draw it and fire a shot on target in a maximum time of two seconds.

The drop-leg holster secures to the belt and leg of the shooter.

Belt Mounted or Drop-Leg

A belt mounted combat holster provides a solid choice. It keeps the weapon secure to the body and allows for rapid access with the dominant hand. Troubles with belt holsters arise when overt body armor clashes with the holster. One of two things may happen. The holstered pistol causes the body armor to ride up or the armor covers the pistol and prevents rapid access. Neither scenario works.

The drop-leg holster secures to the belt and leg of the shooter. This set up lowers the holster body so it is clear of the armor and rapidly accessible to the shooter. All quality drop-leg holsters have adjustable leg straps to vary the height and drop position.

Novice shooters run into trouble when they fail to understand the purpose of the height adjustment. Many new drop-leg holster wearers strap the rig low on their legs so that the rig almost touches the knee. The holster flops around while running or walking quickly and bangs into everything.

The proper method to adjust the height of a drop-leg holster is to put on the overt armor carrier. Adjust the height so the pistol clears the bottom edge of the armor carrier. Test the process by putting on your holster. Stand up straight and allow your arms to hang naturally to the side. The bottom of the holster should be no lower than the tip of you middle finger. If so, then shorten the adjustment straps.

Practice, Practice, Practice

You need to be as familiar and confident with the rig as possible. If you switch from one type of retention system to another, you will have to reprogram your neuromuscular impulses. Under stress, your body will perform exactly as you taught it. You cannot teach yourself to do something new under the pressure of an adrenaline dump.

When you purchase or receive a new holster, it is a good idea to dry-practice with the rig. A few thousand repetitions should overcome your previous muscular habits and instill new skills.

Remember, when you need your pistol in a crisis, you need it instantaneously. The life you save with dedicated practice may be your own.

» Competition Holsters

The holster, a device used to keep the handgun at the ready, can be as simple or as complex as the shooter desires, which includes holsters used for shooting sports competition.

Manufacturers design competition holsters for contests or games. They are not to be confused with holsters used for concealed-carry use.

Respect

A competition or race holster by its very nature is a specialty item. Holster makers purpose build these holsters to shave fractions of seconds from the time score of the competitor. Shooters must afford a great deal of care and respect to the race rig. Sloppy gun handling with a competition holster may lead to a disaster.

Here's the straight-up fact about using a competition holster. Before use, the shooter absolutely must understand the nuances of its design. That understanding must happen before stepping up to the playing field. Failure to do so is amateurish and irresponsible.

How to Choose

Competitions or shooting games vary greatly. Cowboy Action Shooting and the Steel Challenge are both popular shooting games, yet gear requirements are naturally quite different for each.

In some competitions, the shooter moves quickly from one position to another with a holstered gun. In other contests, the shooter moves between stages and begins and ends inside a box with no travel required.

Most of the time, the only requirement of the game is to draw and shoot as fast as possible. In this scenario, shooters hardly concern themselves with holster retention and security. However, if the shooter must run from one station to another before drawing the pistol, retention and security prove a definite concern. These are all questions you must ask yourself when shopping for a competition holster.

What to Choose

If you are new to a particular shooting game, it pays to survey experienced competitors about their choice of holster make and model. Some shooters may find competition holsters expensive. A used holster is worth only a fraction of its purchase price. Save money and frustration by making inquiries first before you make a potentially expensive purchase.

Where to Buy

The competition holster category includes numerous makers. Beretta, Blade-Tech, Comp-Tac and Safariland all have race rigs in their catalogs. You can expect to pay up to $200 for a quality competition rig that is both adjustable and secure.

When searching for a quality competition holster you will come across a wide variety. Several criteria exist that you should keep in mind before making your purchase.

Secure and Adjustable

The term "secure" does not always define gun retention, security systems or the holster fastened tightly to the body. A good competition holster needs to be rigid and stiff so that it does not shift or move about on the shooter's body.

Precious fractions of seconds waste away if the shooter's hand goes down for the pistol and it has somehow shifted or moved. If the gun has moved, it can slow the shooter from getting the proper shooting grip. Fractions of seconds can mean the difference between a first place trophy and a third place showing. The top competitors in the shooting sports always remain fractions of seconds away from each other.

A good competition holster should also adjust to fit the individual body size of the user. The rig should not simply adjust up and down or side to side, but also the cant or angle of the rig should adjust. You will attempt to fit the holster to your very specific body size and arm length.

When properly secure and adjusted, a quality competition rig should feel like a natural extension of your body. The shooting hand should fall directly onto the pistol's grip naturally, without any extra or unnecessary movement.

The Belt

Attaching an expensive competition holster to a cheap belt is ridiculous and amateurish. When you choose your holster you need to put as much consideration into the belt. A competition belt will be very stiff yet offers generous size adjustments.

The holster should fit onto the belt snuggly with no slop or play between them. Expect to pay about fifty percent of the cost of the holster on the belt.

Also, on the topic of belts, you may wish to invest in some belt keepers. A belt keeper is simply a thin strap device with either snaps or Velcro. It is used to secure the overt, external belt to the pant or trouser belt below. Using two to four belt keepers will ensure the gun belt stays securely fastened to the trouser belt and ergonomically to the shooter's body. The combination of quality holster, stiff belt and belt keepers will place the pistol exactly where the shooter needs it to be, all the time.

Practice, Practice, Practice

Far too many new competitors try to go faster than their skill level allows. They outrun their headlights, so to speak and end up having negligent discharges. Often, these acts of negligence result in injury.

A dedicated regiment of dry-fire practice with a twice-checked, unloaded pistol is an absolute must. Dedicated competitors who make their living competing dry-practice for hours at a time. Both Max Michel (World Speed Shooting Champ) and Todd Jarrett (Champion Competitor) stated in separate conversations that they began their careers spending two to three hours a day conducting dry-fire practice.

"When it comes to dry-fire practice, deliberately keep it smooth and methodical, says Max Michel. I try to go about fifty percent of competition speed. That builds the neuromuscular pathways and teaches my body to do it right, not just fast.

He continues, "If the skill is there, your body will be able to go fast. If you don't have the skill it doesn't matter how fast you try to go."

Those are wise words from a man crowned the fastest shooter in the world.

10: Reloading with Magazines

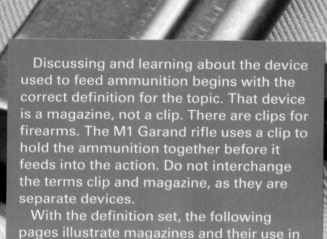

Discussing and learning about the device used to feed ammunition begins with the correct definition for the topic. That device is a magazine, not a clip. There are clips for firearms. The M1 Garand rifle uses a clip to hold the ammunition together before it feeds into the action. Do not interchange the terms clip and magazine, as they are separate devices.

With the definition set, the following pages illustrate magazines and their use in handguns.

Detachable Handgun Magazines

While a few handguns with fixed, non-removable magazines exist, the vast majority of semi-automatic pistols use detachable magazines. There are two types: single-stack and double-stack magazines. The M1911-style magazine is likely the most popular single-stack magazine. Glock produces the most popular double-stack magazines.

Other manufacturers produce numerous aftermarket magazines for modern semi-automatic pistols. Factory magazines historically give better service life, although third-party magazines work in many pistols. However, in the interest of keeping it simple, you will get the best reliability from magazines made by the manufacturer.

Glock produces the most popular double-stack magazines.

Loading and Reloading

Use the same method for loading and reloading single- and double-stack magazines. The following illustrates the method that the author (Paul Markel) has practiced and taught to literally thousands of U.S. military troops during the last several years.

The semi-automatic pistol with a reciprocating slide, refreshes the chamber by the action of the slide cycling to the rear. A cartridge or case ejects, if applicable, and rides forward stripping a fresh round from the magazine and loading it into the chamber.

The dominant hand holds the pistol at approximately eye level. The elbow of the dominant arm rests against the rib cage. If an empty or partial magazine remains in the pistol, activate the magazine release button and let it fall free to the ground. You can secure it later.

Retrieve a loaded magazine with the support hand from a pouch or other area. Do this as the old magazine drops out. Preferably, place the index finger of the support hand straight along the forward edge of the magazine with the tip of the finger touching the top cartridge in the magazine.

Insert the magazine firmly into the magazine well of the gun without slapping or smacking it in. The palm of the support hand should firmly press the magazine until it locks in place. Resist the urge to tap or slap a seated magazine, as this wastes time and effort.

Reach up and over the slide with the support hand, while holding the pistol securely with the dominant hand. Regardless as to whether the slide is in battery or locked to the rear, grasp the rear portion of the slide. Pull it rapidly and firmly to the rear. When the slide reaches the limit of travel, release it and allow the power of the recoil spring to close the action. Resist the urge to ride the slide home with the support hand.

The gun should now have a fresh round of ammunition in the chamber, a loaded magazine in place and be ready to fire. If for some reason this action did not chamber a round, the magazine may be defective or dirty.

The method remains the same regardless of whether you are initially loading an empty gun, reloading a gun that has just run dry or fully charging a gun that has a partially depleted magazine. This method works whether the slide is forward or to the rear.

Numerous other ways or methods exist to charge a handgun. No matter the choice, you should practice repetition throughout the process. When forced to recharge a gun under stress, if you have taught yourself to perform three different tasks, your mind must first decide which task is most appropriate for the situation. Time is not likely something of which you will have a great deal during a gunfight.

Retrieve a magazine with support hand. Place the forefinger along the front edge.

Securely insert the magazine into the magazine well.

Seat the magazine with the palm of the hand. Resist the urge to tap or slap it.

Reach up and over and grasp rear of the slide.

Pull the slide to the limit of travel and release.

Magazine Maintenance and Repair

Of all the parts on the semi-automatic handgun, few surpass the magazine in order of importance. If the magazine fails, you essentially have a single-shot pistol. Although it is generally unwise to oil or lubricate the springs of your magazines, we recommend that you disassemble them from time to time to clear out the normal dust and dirt. An all-purpose brush and cotton rag are all you should need.

If you ever submerge your magazines in water or subject them to sand and mud, you must take them apart as soon as it is practical to do so. Magazine springs and bodies can and will rust.

Of all the components on the semi-automatic handgun that you may have to replace, the magazine is the simplest. If you have a magazine that is giving you problems, get rid of it and replace it with a new one. Bad magazines are not worth the hassle and could cost you your life in a fight. Think of magazines as replaceable components, they are not meant to last forever.

11: Speedloaders

In the world of firearms, revolvers define reliability and simplicity. No other handgun is more easily manipulated or dependable. All of these traits make revolvers a no-brainer for concealed carry. However, deciding which gun is best for you is a battle of tradeoffs.

Small capacity (often six shots) and difficulty reloading remain detractors and points of concern when considering revolvers as viable defense weapons. However, speedloaders make reloading nearly as fast as slipping a fresh magazine into an autoloader.

Speed loaders are the best way to quickly reload your revolver.

Knowing you are able to quickly reload your revolver instills confidence.

Speedloader Logic

Speedloaders are the best and fastest way to reload a spent revolver. They're small, easy to use and cheap. A simple twist of the contraption gives you another cylinder's worth of ammo, whether that is five, six, seven or more shots.

The bulk of revolvers hold six bullets, hence the nicknames "six-gun" and "six-shooter." The caliber and size of the gun largely determine how many bullets will fit into the cylinder, but as a rule, the bigger the bullet, the bigger the cylinder and gun. When a bullet fires, immense pressure is put on the cylinder's wall as the case expands from the burning powder. If the walls are too thin, they will crack or fail completely. This is why you need to be cognizant of the pressure rating for your gun. If you choose to shoot ammunition designated as having higher pressure (+P), make sure your gun can handle it.

Smaller, lower pressure revolvers like .22 LR chambered guns often have capacities nearing 10 rounds. Most defensive revolvers hold five to seven rounds. While this doesn't sound like much, keep in mind that with just one speedloader you can double your gun's capacity.

Most speedloaders work very similarly. A knob on the back controls a star-shaped dial that holds the cartridges in place. Turn it one way and the bullets are secure. Rotating it the opposite direction releases the bullets.

It's important to know that speedloaders are not the most secure means of holding ammo. They're still the best option for filling your revolver in a hurry, but they'll likely come out of the loader if carried freely in your pocket. Many stores offer pouches that ride on your belt keeping speedloaders secure and at the ready. HKS makes affordable options while Safariland offers a bit nicer and sturdier models.

Loading With Speedloaders

Speedloaders are easy to use, but using them quickly requires practice. With practice comes fluidity and speed, but in their use — especially early on — slower is often faster. If you get in too big of a rush, you will fumble the whole process and find yourself stabbing the bullets at the empty cylinder.

Start by having your speedloader ready to go. Your pocket isn't a good choice for carrying a speedloader day-to-day. A pouch is the best option because they keep loaders in just the right position and hold them secure and hidden until needed. They will sit along your strong side and can look a little out of place if left in the open, but there's no extra permit needed to carry them. It's best to hide them under a light jacket or T-shirt. The most common options hold one or two loaders.

To refill a revolver quickly, first empty the gun. Release the cylinder, point the gun skyward and swat the ejector rod with your non-shooting hand to dump the spent brass. After the brass is clear, immediately point the gun at the ground. Undo the flap of the pouch, grab the speedloader by the circular body and guide it into place, releasing the knob. Then, snap the cylinder shut again. This is the fastest method of using a speedloader, and also the most natural. Practice enough so that your time from opening the cylinder to closing it is about four seconds.

After you fire your last shot, swing the cylinder open.

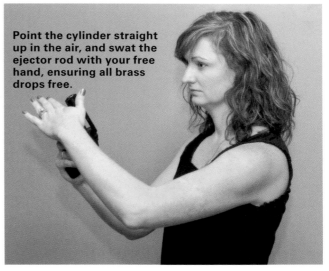

Point the cylinder straight up in the air, and swat the ejector rod with your free hand, ensuring all brass drops free.

Once you've ensured the cylinder is empty, point the gun back at the ground and grab your speedloader.

Seat the loader firmly into the cylinder.

Twist the knob to drop the bullets free.

Speed Strips

Speedloaders and their pouches can have a bulky appearance. Many shooters favor a slimmer alternative called a speed strip. Rather than hold the bullets in a shape that mimics your gun's cylinder, speed strips hold the bullets in a straight line. They are not quite as fast as a speed-loader and require a few more movements, but with practice, you can learn to use them quickly. A speed strip pouch looks similar to a cell phone pouch, so concealment is a non-issue.

Empty your gun in the aforementioned fashion (point up, swat, point down) and then draw your speed strip from your belt. It is best to load only five bullets onto a strip so you have a larger area to grab; otherwise, you are relying on a tiny tab of plastic for grip. Wrap your middle finger around the empty section of the strip. Then lay your thumb down on the bullets on one side of the strip and your index finger along the top. Now you have a solid hold of the strip for fast and accurate manipulation. You're going to be loading two bullets at a time. Once you get the first pair in the cylinder, roll your hand forward along the length of the strip to pop them free and then rotate the cylinder with the thumb of the hand that's holding the gun and repeat.

If neither a speedloader nor speedstrip tickles your fancy, ammo dump pouches that hold loose shells may be an alternative. Regardless of whether you use speed strips, speedloaders or an ammo dump pouch, it's essential to have spare ammunition on hand if you choose to carry a revolver.

Speed strips are an alternative to speedloaders. While not as fast to implement, they are easier to conceal.

RUGER LCR

38 SPL +P

02827

121

12: Calibers and Ammunition

Modern calibers come in a host of different sizes and energy loads that accommodate both self-defense and practice shooting.

Bullets and gunpowder have evolved significantly since black powder guns sporadically fired lead balls from somewhat straight barrels. Today, we have smokeless powder that sends expanding hollow-point bullets zipping down precision rifled barrels. It's this smokeless powder that allows us to get big performance out of small guns and calibers. Today, rounds like the .380 ACP are enjoying power levels that were unheard of even a decade ago, making it a viable self-defense round.

No matter the caliber of bullet you choose to protect yourself with, you must be able to shoot it competently. A .22 LR to the center mass of a target is more effective at stopping a threat than a .45 in the arm. Bullet selection is a macho show for some packers. For this crowd, nothing less than a .45 ACP will do. If there were a .46-caliber option available, they'd pack that. The flip side of this argues that a well-placed .45 is more effective at neutralizing a threat than the same well-placed .22. Armed citizens have a plethora of choices in ammunition.

The rimfire .22 LR should be avoided as a self-defense round unless the shooter is extremely sensitive to recoil.

.22 Long Rifle

The .22 LR (Long Rifle), a very common caliber, is not a round commonly used for self-defense. Many people argue a .38 caliber is the minimum cartridge a shooter should use. However, suppose you cannot shoot a .38 worth a darn. If you feel unsure about the gun, chances are you will not carry it.

You will not find a shortage of handguns chambered in .22. Guns for self-defense range from small revolvers to even smaller derringers and all the way up to high-capacity autoloaders. If you choose a .22, ensure your gun functions flawlessly with your carry ammunition of choice. A rule of thumb for reliability is 500 jam-free rounds with minimal cleaning. The nature of the tiny, rimmed .22 cartridge often proves problematic in small autoloaders. Some of these guns have delicate actions, which is not a desirable trait in defense weapons where reliability is paramount.

As far as stopping power goes, the .22 offers roughly 100 to 150 foot-pounds of energy, depending on the type. Energy on target, calculated as kinetic energy, is the amount of "oomph" a bullet delivers when it hits a target. The greater the kinetic energy, the more shock a bullet has upon impact. The shock is what stops threats cold.

The anemic .25 ACP should be avoided as a self-defense round, as its ballistics are worse than the .22 and the round is expensive and difficult to find.

.25 ACP

The .25 ACP is the smallest centerfire round for handguns commercially available today. Its small size and low recoil make it a good chambering for small autoloaders. The ACP — in all ACP calibers — stands for Automatic Colt Pistol, a reference for the guns they were initially chambered for, such as the .45 ACP.

The tiny .25 is not suitable for self-defense for a number of reasons. First and foremost is the round's ballistics. Despite utilizing a larger-diameter bullet (projectile) than a .22 LR (.251 vs. .223), its performance worsens due to a short case and increased bullet weight. A shooter is better off with a .22 than a .25. Also, .25 ammunition is scarce, choices are limited and if you find any, it's typically more expensive than more common and more effective rounds like the 9mm.

In a typical gun chambered for .25, you can expect anywhere from 63 to 94 foot-pounds of kinetic energy from bullets weighing between 35 and 50 grains. In comparison, the 9mm can offer upwards of 500 foot-pounds in hot 124-grain loadings.

There are few guns chambered for .25. One of the most famous is the Beretta 418, James Bond's sidearm in the pre-*Dr. No* novels. Bond also used a .32 ACP, Walther PPK .380 and a .40 S&W. Like the famous spy, it's wise to consider other calibers as well.

.32 H&R Magnum and .327 Federal Magnum

The .32 H&R Magnum is a rimmed cartridge designed for use in revolvers. Developed in 1984 as a joint venture between Harrington & Richardson and Federal Cartridge, the .32 H&R Magnum is produced by lengthening the .32 S&W Long case by 0.155-inch, to 1.075 inches.

The .32 H&R magnum offers substantially more performance than other .32 caliber handgun cartridges, such as the .32 ACP. Considered an effective small game hunting cartridge, it offers marginal effectiveness as a self-defense round. Its higher velocity offers a flat trajectory, while the light weight of the bullets results in low recoil. The older .32-20 Winchester was extremely popular in the Winchester lever-action rifles and Colt single-actions, available at the turn of the century, for small-to-medium game hunting and self defense. The .32 H&R offers near duplicate performance.

One of the .32 H&R Magnum's favorable attributes is that it offers .38 Special energy levels and allows a small-frame revolver to hold six cartridges, whereas a similarly sized revolver in .38 special would only hold five rounds. Greater penetration for the .32 H&R Magnum compared to the .38 special with bullets of the same weight, gives it a slight edge.

The .327 Federal Magnum is based on the .32 H&R Magnum and improves performance to levels near that of the .357 Magnum.

The .327 Federal Magnum is a cartridge introduced by Sturm, Ruger and Federal Cartridge, intended to provide the power of a .357 Mag-

The .327 Federal Magnum rivals the .357 Magnum in performance, but has less recoil.

num in six-shot, compact revolvers, whose cylinders only hold five rounds of the larger .357 Magnum cartridge. The .327 Federal Magnum is actually a super magnum, having replaced the .32 H&R Magnum as the top performer of the cartridge diameter.

The .327 Federal Magnum is an attempt to improve on the .32 H&R Magnum, introduced in 1984, a round which failed to attract shooters or manufacturers. This is the third updated version of the original .32 S&W cartridge, which dates back to 1878. The original was a black powder cartridge with a case length of 0.610-inch, which developed a velocity of approximately 700 fps. The first improvement of the round came in 1896 with the introduction of the .32 S&W Long, which had a case length of 0.920 in and generated slightly higher velocities. The introduction of the .32 H&R Magnum nearly a century later increased the case length to 1.075-inch and pushed the pressure up from the very low 15,000 psi to 21,000 psi CUP, which is similar to .38 Special +P. This gave velocities of greater than 1,200 fps, a respect-

able increase, but was not enough to garner any great interest in the cartridge.

Based on the .32 H&R Magnum, stretched and loaded to a higher pressure of 45,000 psi. (Of note, the standard pressure .44 Magnum is 36,000 psi), the .327, with an actual bullet diameter of 0.312-inch, achieves velocities up to 1,400 fps with 100-grain bullets and up to 1,300 fps with 115-grain bullets, from the 3 1/16-inch barreled Ruger SP-101 revolver.

The small framed Ruger SP-101 chambered in the .327 Federal Magnum was released in January 2008. Currently, most of the factory loads on the market are designed for self-defense in short barrels, but with a load pressure of a 45,000 psi, velocities can be expected to increase with heavier, hotter loads designed for hunting.

Revolvers chambered for the .327 Federal Magnum can also fire the .327 H&R Magnum, the .32 S&W and the .32 S&W Long.

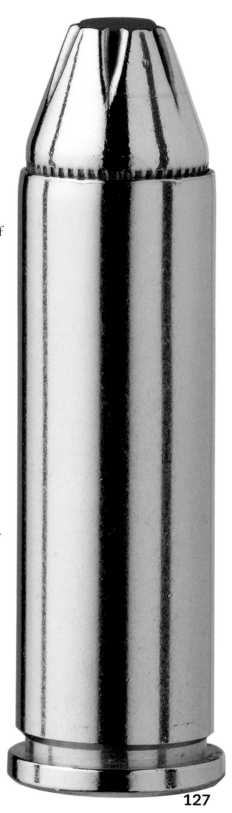

.32 ACP

The .32 ACP, slightly more common than the .25 for self-defense, is seen as underpowered by the gun community at large. In Europe, it's known as the 7.62x17mm Browning SR, in honor of its inventor, John Moses Browning. 7.62 is the metric measurement of the bullet's diameter, while 17mm represents the case length in millimeters.

The .32 fires a .301-caliber projectile (the .32-inch specification comes from the diameter of the case) at a meager 900 or so fps, which offers downrange energy in the neighborhood of 125 foot-pounds. Most .32 bullets weigh either 65 or 71 grains, not quite up to snuff when it comes to effectively stopping a threat cold. However, Buffalo Bore Ammunition, known for their hot loads, created a .32 load that registers 220 foot-pounds of energy. It's a +P round, which means it fires at a higher pressure than most .32 loads, so it's best to check your weapon first to see if it's made to handle the increased pressure. If nothing indicates this on the firearm itself, it's wise to stay away from +P.

It is best to opt for the largest caliber you are comfortable with and can shoot proficiently. When you feel comfortable with your gun, you will carry it. If .32-level recoil is all you can stand, start shopping for a .32. Kel-Tec's P32, the Beretta Tomcat and the Seecamp LWS are popular guns chambered in .32, with the Kel-Tec being the most affordable of the three. All three are reliable and easily fit in a purse or pocket.

The .32 is a very marginal round for self-defense. Most shooters who carry a small cartridge opt for the .380 ACP or 9mm Luger.

.380 ACP

The .380 has seen a massive resurgence in recent years, thanks to skyrocketing numbers of concealed carry licenses nationwide. A plethora of small pocket guns followed — many chambered in .380 — and the tiny weapons became a premium commodity. All the major manufacturers released .380 guns and most offer great options for concealed carry. Popular options include Smith & Wesson's Bodyguard .380, which has a built-in laser, the Kel-Tec P3AT and Sig Sauer's P238. Classic .380 guns include the Seecamp and Walther PPK.

Most shooters consider the .380 a minimum for an effective self-defense weapon. Scores of articles exist on the .380's terminal performance, and all point to the same conclusion: having a .380 is better than not having a gun, but just barely. The .380 bears a projectile that's the same diameter as the 9mm (.351 inches), but the case is shorter, which means it offers less power, even in higher-pressure +P loadings. Not every firearm can handle the increased pressure offered by +P loads. However, when using smaller caliber rounds, +P is a wise choice if you can handle the increase in recoil. Buffalo Bore's .380 +P offers nearly 300 foot-pounds of kinetic energy from an 80-grain projectile.

The main selling point of most guns chambered for .380 remains their size. All the aforementioned pistols easily pack in a pocket or purse and are very light, with the exception of the steel-framed Walther. Since many shooters prefer the .380, ammunition makers produce many effective self-defense loads for these small guns. Special blends of powder burn fast and are ideal for short barrels, as many .380 guns have barrels in the 2-inch range. Hornady's Critical Defense and Remington's Golden Saber bullets remain top choices among the concealed carry crowd for their excellent expansion in soft tissue.

.38 Smith & Wesson Special

The most popular option in self-defense revolvers is the .38 Special. Smith & Wesson developed this caliber in 1898, hence its official moniker, the .38 Smith & Wesson Special. The earliest incarnation used black powder, which eventually switched to smokeless powder because of its popularity, smoke-free nature and improved performance. Autoloaders were years away from widespread acceptance, and revolvers were the weapon of choice for everyone from outlaws to law enforcement.

The .38 Special features a rimmed casing, as most revolver-specific cartridges do, so the bullets can "hang" onto the outside of the cylinder. It has straight walls (no bottleneck), as did most loads from that period . A relatively low-pressure round, the .38 continues as one of the best-selling rounds today due to its effectiveness and never-ending popularity.

The .38 is also one of the most inherently accurate rounds available, which is why many target shooters rely on the .38. Many shooters also favor the .38 due to the wide range of options in loaded ammunition. Though the bullet is called the .38 Special, the bullet fired is a .357-inch projectile. The .38-inch measurement comes from the diameter of the case when wrapped around the bullet rather than the bullet itself. Most .38 Special loads have a bullet weighing anywhere from 90 to 158 grains, though you may find odd-balls both above and below this range. The mildest .38 loads send the bullet easing along at 600 or so feet per second, while hot +P+ loads can rival light .357 Magnum power at a sizzling 1,100 fps.

Just about every shooter can effectively manage the recoil from standard-pressure .38 rounds. The +P offerings add negligible muzzle jump and recoil despite the improved ballistics and terminal performance. A "snubby," or snub-nosed revolver, named because of its short barrel, is any revolver with a barrel three inches or shorter. Some shooters favor the Smith & Wesson Model 642 or 442 for concealed carry because of their hammerless design and light weight. Both models offer five round capacity and unquestioned reliability, like many revolvers.

Any reputable ammunition maker makes at least several .38 Special offerings from cast lead, full metal jacket target loads to full-house hollow points. Manufacturers provide shooters with many ammunition choices. Many of the larger manufacturers feature fast-burning powder that offers a low-flash signature and improved performance from short barrels. Hornady's Critical Defense and Remington's Golden Saber and Speer's Gold Dot hollow points are common favorites of law enforcement and armed citizens.

This is a go-to for many revolver shooters. Its popularity over the years is unequaled.

The 9mm Luger is the most ubiquitous handgun cartridge on the planet and for good reason: it's cheap, effective, recoil is very manageable — even in small guns — and 9mm-chambered guns often enjoy high capacity.

9mm Luger

The 9mm Luger, also known by its metric measurements 9X19 Parabellum and simply 9mm, is one of the most popular cartridges among the concealed carry crowd. Shooters favor the 9mm Luger because of its effectiveness, low recoil and affordability.

The 9mm Luger gets its namesake from its German inventor. A pistol would later bear that same name as the German sidearm for much of the early 20th century. Today it's the standard sidearm round for NATO forces, which is why the American military made the switch from the .45 ACP-chambered M1911 pistol and went with the 9mm-chambered Beretta M9. The M9 is still the standard sidearm for most of the U.S. military.

While the 9mm remains one of the most common rounds on the planet, it still has its detractors. Some instructors and gun scribes say an acceptable round for self-defense must have a caliber that starts with a '4' and the .40 Smith & Wesson is the minimum, with the ideal being .45 ACP. Scores of data from ballistics tests and real-world reports from military and police say otherwise. Bigger is not always better.

The 9mm launches a .351-inch projectile (identical to the .380 ACP) and creates kinetic energy levels from the high 300s to nearly 500 foot-pounds. Velocities in the 1,500 fps range are also not uncommon because the 9mm has a higher pressure round than any of the previous cartridges. Loads denoted +P have an even higher pressure. Most 9mm bullets fall in the range of 95 to 147 grains.

Many handgun manufacturers, large and small, offer guns chambered for 9mm. Although the 9mm remains popular in the law enforcement community, the larger and more powerful .40 Smith & Wesson is making inroads. Most 9mm carry guns, like the Smith & Wesson M&P line and many others, have large capacities (usually 15 or more per magazine) and are still concealable. Other popular carry choices include the Glock 19, Sig Sauer P938, Ruger LC9 and Kahr CM9. A bullet like the 9mm does not require an especially beefy action or frame, so it's at home in pocket guns as well as full-size offerings. Recoil in smaller guns is more pronounced than in the heavier, full-size models, but it's nothing that can't be learned and managed.

Consider this the next time you hear or read someone criticizing the 9mm: If it is good enough for our military and law enforcement, isn't it good enough for you?

.40 Smith & Wesson

This is a step up from the 9mm Luger, both in power and recoil. Hot .40 loads can be tough to manage in smaller pistols, though recoil can be learned and managed.

The .40 Smith & Wesson came about by way of a downsizing from its parent case, the 10mm Auto. Designers devised this round to create a rimless handgun cartridge with stopping power on par with the .357 Magnum, but in a round chambered for autoloading pistols. The round's designers achieved what they wanted — the 10mm is a veritable wrecking ball in the handgun world. Around the same time, the FBI wanted to adopt a new cartridge with more power than their current service revolvers, so they tested the 10mm.

Ballistically, the 10mm is a marvel. The 10mm penetrates deep and expands exceptionally well because of its high velocity. However, one problem arose, recoil was a bear and many FBI agents could not pass the agency's pistol course with this caliber. Consequently, by retaining the .40-caliber projectile from the 10mm, Smith & Wesson and Winchester collaborated and shortened the 10mm's case. While the .40 S&W fits in guns with 9mm-sized frames and actions, the 10mm requires a beefy frame and larger gun.

The .40 S&W is a popular choice among law enforcement agencies, enjoying a distribution slightly less than that of the 9mm. Popular loads fire a .40-caliber projectile in the 135- to 200-grain range anywhere from 1,000 to 1,300 fps. Most harbor a kinetic energy of 420 to 500 foot-pounds. The heavy +P load from Buffalo Bore launches a 155-grain projectile at 1,300 fps for 582 foot-pounds.

Recoil is challenging in lighter guns. The .40 S&W features a snappier recoil than that of the .38 Special or 9mm Luger because of its higher pressure load. You must practice to become proficient at taming a gun's recoil.

Shooters have a wealth of acceptable .40 S&W self-defense loads available to choose from. Most loads feature hollow-point projectiles or expanding flat points, also called soft points. Before you choose a particular load to carry in your gun, ensure that your weapon functions flawlessly with it for no less than 200 rounds, though 500 is the suggested benchmark.

.45 ACP

The .45 ACP has a well-earned reputation as an effective man stopper, even with non-expanding full metal jacket (FMJ) bullets. From 1911 through the early 1980s, our troops used these cast copper jacketed lead slugs in their M1911 pistols. The infamous Thompson Submachine Gun (Tommy Gun) fired .45 ACP rounds housed inside its menacing drum magazine.

The .452-diameter projectile is larger than any other common self-defense round. If you add an expanding hollow point or soft point bullet, you have a veritable threat stopper, as these bullets create cavernous wound channels in soft tissue. Guns chambered for the .45 ACP range from full-size, high-capacity autoloaders to tiny single-stack pocket guns. Shooters have many choices because of the caliber's popularity. Many find the .45's recoil easy to handle. Of course, lighter guns produce more pronounced recoil and muzzle blast.

Most .45 loads fall between 160 and 230 grains and have energy levels near 600 foot-pounds in hot loads. Muzzle velocities north of 1,100 fps are also common in barrels four inches or longer.

This is the big-bore offering highly praised by defense experts. When it comes to one-shot stopping power with manageable recoil, look no further.

.357 Sig

This relative newcomer is based off of the .40 S&W. The engineers at firearms manufacturer SIG Sauer wanted a high-velocity bullet that improved on the performance of the 9mm Luger, but didn't require a larger gun to handle. So, they necked down (shrunk) the .40 S&W case to accept a .355-inch diameter bullet, which would send velocities well north of most pistol rounds. Bullet weights are most similar to 9mm weights, typically in the 115- to 147-grain range. Velocities commonly exceed 1,500 fps in hot +P offerings, with kinetic energy reaching greater than 600 foot-pounds. This scorcher defines the term 'pocket rocket.'

Some police agencies adopted the .357 Sig, but not en masse as some hoped. The cost of .357 Sig remains higher than that of .40 simply because of less commonality and fewer guns chamber this round. The .357 Sig has greater penetration than most handgun loads because of its scorching velocities.

Since the .357 Sig's case is based off of the .40 S&W, all you need to fire a .357 Sig from a gun chambered in .40 S&W is a barrel change. Shooters can find many conversion kits available, especially for Glock firearms. The .357 and .40 have the same magazines and they both handle high-pressure loads. If you can handle the snappy recoil and noise, the .357 Sig proves worthy of investigating as a self-defense round.

This blisteringly fast round offers snappy recoil, a loud bark and lots of kinetic energy downrange.

10mm Automatic

This beefed-up .40-caliber round represents the pinnacle in straight-walled autoloader performance and ballistics. However, like all hot and heavy pistol loads, high velocity and terminal performance produces considerable recoil. The very fact that many trained law enforcement officers struggled with the recoil of full-house 10mm loads should clue you in to the level of muzzle flip. However, a cult following of 10mm lovers accept nothing less. These people swear that the S&W in .40 S&W stands for "Short & Wimpy."

Most bullets found in 10mm cases range between 135 and 180 grains, but 200 grain loads are available. The 10mm produces exceptional Kinetic energy, with the upper echelon 10mm rounds flirting with 750 foot-pounds of energy, right on par with the best .357 Magnum loads. Generally a higher pressure round than the .357, the 10mm can achieve these kinds of numbers.

Most guns chambered for 10mm are full-size handguns because of the hot nature of the round, though Glock's model 29 is a subcompact. Glock, EAA and Colt offer solid 10mm handguns, while perhaps the most famous and attractive 10mm ever is Colt's Delta Elite 1911-style pistol.

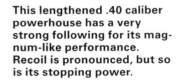

This lengthened .40 caliber powerhouse has a very strong following for its magnum-like performance. Recoil is pronounced, but so is its stopping power.

.357 Smith & Wesson Magnum

The .357 Magnum came about from a law enforcement need in the early 1900s when their .38 Special loads would not penetrate the door panels of new automobiles. Manufacturers lengthened the .38's case and the projectile remained the same, a .357-inch diameter lead bullet. If you decide you want a revolver for personal defense, consider one with a .357 Magnum chambering; you can shoot everything from light .38 Special loads all the way up to full-house .357 loads if you decide the .38 is not enough.

Many shooters favor the .357 Magnum as an effective self-defense load. It combines heavy bullets with high velocities, the formula for effective stopping power. However, along with this comes plenty of noise, muzzle blast and recoil. Most bullets fall within the 110- to 170-grain range, though 200-grain loads are available. At the upper end of performance, Buffalo Bore's 125-grain offering sizzles at 1,400-plus fps and harbors a massive 783 foot-pounds of kinetic energy. You can purchase faster loads, but the law of diminishing returns might apply here; you get more velocity, but is it worth the additional recoil and blast?

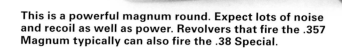

This is a powerful magnum round. Expect lots of noise and recoil as well as power. Revolvers that fire the .357 Magnum typically can also fire the .38 Special.

.44 Remington Magnum

Biblical recoil. Deafening muzzle blast. Unparalleled man-stopping ability. These three traits describe the .44 Magnum in a nutshell. The .44 Magnum is also one of the most famous calibers. In the 1971 film "Dirty Harry," Clint Eastwood brandishes the new-at-the-time Smith & Wesson Model 29, a long-barreled six-gun that his character, Inspector Harry Callahan, proclaims as "the most powerful handgun in the world." Though the .454 Casull and .500 Smith & Wesson Magnum have since surpassed the .44 Magnum in terms of kinetic energy, most still consider the .44 a veritable hammer.

Some may find it difficult to easily conceal and carry a .44 Magnum. Most .44 Magnum's incorporate large frames to absorb some of the substantial recoil that even light loads produce. Though they exist in the form of the 2-inch barreled Smith & Wesson Model 629, many shooters simply can't handle the recoil offered by a packable-sized .44 Magnum. Emptying a 5-shot cylinder of a .44 snubby generates enough force to make you cognizant of every tendon and muscle in your wrist. However, much like the relationship between the .38 and .357 Magnum, a shorter, less powerful .44 load is available; the .44 Special. The .44 Special creates less recoil and blast, but still offers the big .44-caliber bullet.

Though it's called the .44 Magnum and Special, the bullets are .429 inch in diameter. Common bullet weights are 180 grains all the way up to 340 grains, which best suit hunting applications. Kinetic energy of the .44 Magnum will make even the hottest .357 Magnum blush; a +P+ Buffalo Bore heavy .44 load pushes 1,700 foot-pounds of energy. Needless to say, firing such a bullet isn't for the faint of heart or weak of wrist.

If you're set on packing one of the most effective man stoppers around and are willing to accept the recoil, the .44 might just be for you.

This is considered the upper end of what's reasonably packable in a carry gun. In hot loads, the recoil is punishing and the report deafening, but nothing previously mentioned comes close to the stopping power that the big .44 packs.

Odds and ends

The previously mentioned rounds are the most common for self-defense, but are by no means the only viable choices. Scores of other calibers exist that armed citizens rely on, but they're simply not as popular. Here are a few other choices.

.45 GAP

Glock introduced this .45-caliber round as a lighter recoiling alternative to the .45 ACP. Very few police agencies adopted the .45 Glock Automatic Pistol, which has ballistic performance slightly less than that of the .45 ACP. Shooters have limited ammunition options, as the GAP hasn't fared the sort of success Glock imagined it would. Gun options are limited, too. Go figure.

The .45 GAP caliber round really never caught on and is almost commercially sunk.

.38 Super

This round never received popularity worthy of its performance. The .38 round is a high-velocity round based off of the .380 case, but lengthened to accommodate more powder. The .356-inch bullets often leave the barrel at roughly 1,400-plus fps and have energy levels in the 500 foot-pound range, with some exceeding that. This puts the .38 Super in the realm of the venerable .45 ACP and .357 Magnum.

However, a limited selection of defense loads exist for the .38 Super, and it's most commonly known as a competition round.

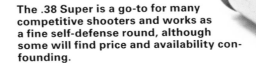

The .38 Super is a go-to for many competitive shooters and works as a fine self-defense round, although some will find price and availability confounding.

.500 Smith & Wesson Magnum

If nothing less than the biggest, gnarliest pistol round will do, then you need the .500 Magnum. The mere sight of this hand cannon should deter criminals from messing with you. If it doesn't, you've got the most powerful commercially available handgun round at your disposal.

Ammo makers produce bullets weighing in at 440 grains that carry astronomically high kinetic energy levels; Buffalo Bore's offering produces almost 2,700 foot-pounds of energy. That's as much as common deer-hunting rifle calibers, but in your hand. Good luck holding on to the gun as it recoils. The half-inch bullet diameter is the largest legally available without a special tax stamp that also regulates machine guns.

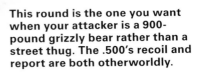

This round is the one you want when your attacker is a 900-pound grizzly bear rather than a street thug. The .500's recoil and report are both otherworldly.

Part III

Training Introduction

Far too often, the shooting community uses the words "training" and "practice" interchangeably.

People say, "I'm going to the range to train." What they really mean to say is they are going to the range to practice.

We will address practice and training as separate topics. Training occurs under the watchful eye of a professional and experienced instructor to gain knowledge and learn new skills. To a lesser extent, it is to affirm the skills and knowledge previously received. In a nutshell, training teaches you how and what to practice.

Practice, on the other hand, is something that you can do on your own. You train at a class or school. You practice at your home range on your own time. Training does not give you the ability to shoot. Training introduces you to the information, methods and techniques. The dedicated practice that you undertake after training is what helps build your skill set.

James Yeager of Tactical Response put it this way. "When you take training, it's like buying a car on payments. Your training course is like the down payment on the car. When you go home, you practice. That is like making monthly payments. Make enough payments and you own the car. Practice enough and you will own the skill you were taught in training. If you stop making payments, they take your car away. If you don't practice after you have taken the training, you lose the skill."

Training seems to be the hardest thing for men to do. There are so many egos tied to gun ownership that many men will not risk their pride by attending training. They fear they will find out they are not as good as they think they are. Just as muscles cannot grow unless you push them to the limit, skill at handling a firearm cannot grow unless you push your limits.

The best way to push your limits and grow your skill is to actually attend a professional training course. If you hope to increase your skill and effectiveness with a firearm, you need to leave the comfort of your little pond and get out into the world. The first step is up to you.

13: Training Methods

Training occurs under the watchful eye of an experienced instructor. Once understood, it's time to consider how students of the gun acquire knowledge and physical skill.

You must consider where and how you will take the training. Choosing an instructor is equally important.

Taking private classes from a qualified instructor better prepares you for real-world scenarios.

Individual Coaching

Taking private classes with a professional instructor provides shooters the opportunity to develop practical shooting skills. However, this takes time and financial means. A good instructor is like a good attorney. They are not just sitting around waiting for the telephone to ring. You need to book your training with them well ahead of time, but they can also assist by working around your schedule.

For quality instruction, expect to pay between $50 and $100 per hour. Avoid instructors with a reduced rate, as this may indicate someone who is not a professional. Students must be dedicated to get the most from the training. Booking a single training session of an hour or two is just the beginning, not the end.

Training is the first step to proper handgun handling. The next step is practice.

Day Trips

If you live in or around a large metropolitan area, you may be fortunate enough to take a training course within commuting distance. Consider yourself fortunate if this is the case. Typically, this requires a road trip away from home.

Professional shooting schools provide a great place to connect with a peer group that supports the same pro-gun, self-defense ideas that you value.

Shooting Adventure

Numerous professional shooting schools with excellent reputations exist across the country. They include Gunsite Academy in Arizona and Texas Pistol Academy. Other schools include Tactical Defense Institute in Ohio, International Tactical Training Seminars in California and the SIG Academy in New Hampshire.

When you decide to enroll in a professional shooting school, view the trip as a "shooting adventure." A trip to a shooting school or academy presents a great opportunity to commune with like-minded individuals. It is beneficial to connect with a peer group that supports the same pro-gun, self-defense ideas that you value.

Often, pro-gun people feel isolated in their beliefs, which can lead to a feeling of isolation and frustration. Thus, enrolling in a professional shooting school provides an environment to interact with individuals with similar beliefs and gain peer affirmation.

Everyone learns skills at their own pace. The key is doing so in a group environment and under the eye of an instructor.

Skill Development and Teaching Methods

Several basic principles apply to teaching and learning, regardless of the skill level. The subject of instruction is relatively immaterial. It doesn't matter if you teach shooting skills, golfing or knitting.

People learn new information in different ways. Instructors must use different methods of teaching to effectively help each student learn in the way that best suits them individually. Some people can read a topic description and easily understand how to perform the related physical task. Others can hear it explained and fully understand the idea. Some people learn best when shown a task on video or in a live demonstration. Finally, some people best grasp a concept by hands-on participation.

When teaching firearms handling and manipulation to a group of students, instructors first explain the task to the students. Next, the instructor slowly and deliberately demonstrates the skill under a dry-fire scenario. In the last step, the instructor demonstrates the skill in real time with real ammunition.

Students then go through those same steps, beginning with the dry-fire session and then with ammo in a loaded gun. In all steps, the instructor observes and critiques the students.

Students will then go through those same steps, beginning with the dry-fire version and then with ammo in a loaded gun. In all steps the student will be observed and critiqued by the instructor.

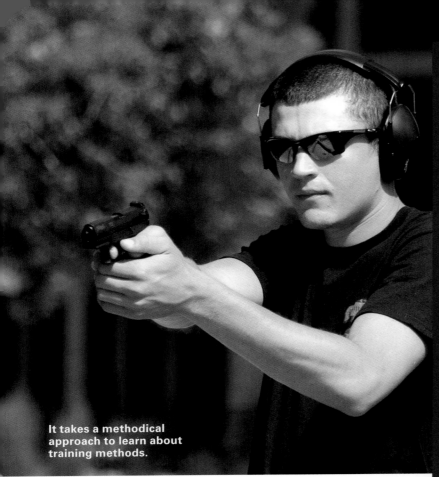

It takes a methodical approach to learn about training methods.

Known to Unknown

Acknowledging the known before moving to the unknown is the most accepted first step for teaching new skills. The instructor must establish a common baseline before teaching the new or unknown. This theory applies to students learning new gun skills. There must be some type of baseline skill set established before advancing the training.

Gun students move from the simple to the complex, after proceeding from the known to the unknown. Students must take several steps before they can expect to engage multiple targets from awkward positions. These steps include making sure you can reliably and repeatedly put rounds into the target from a simple standing position.

Following the steps in a slow, deliberate fashion assures a student can move from basic to intermediate shooting skills.

Student of the Gun University

Paul G. Markel is a full-time small arms and tactics instructor. Readers can benefit from his teaching expertise, specifically in this chapter. Markel wrote this and other chapters in this book.

Markel is uniquely qualified to write and teach as he's done both for many years and continues to do so in many ways. In 1987, he joined the U.S. Marines and then spent 17 years as a police officer in civilian life. Today, he's a book author and host of *Student of the Gun*, an educational and entertain-ment focused TV series on The Sportsman Channel.

As an instructor, Markel introduced handgun and small arms use and tactics to thousands of soldiers in the military. Now, he continues instruction through Student of the Gun University, which

includes a course called "Handgun 101." This instructional series includes intermediate and advanced courses such as Ballistic Problem Solving. Learn more at www.StudentoftheGun.com.

14: Dry-Fire Practice

Practice dry-firing just as you would in a live-fire event, meticulously applying the fundamentals.

When shooters engage in dry-fire practice, they use a firearm without ammunition. All training regimen, including military, follow this practice.

When first introduced to using a rifle, service members spend long hours and days on the firing line. The gun is not loaded with a live round for a reason. Paul Markel, one of this book's authors, is a former U.S. Marine. His dry-fire experience punctuates the benefits of dry-fire practice for every shooter.

"During basic training we spent an entire week dry-firing with our M16A2 rifles. Our instructors combined verbal teaching methods with hours upon hours of dedicated dry-fire drills. We were assured that if we dedi-cated ourselves to the dry-fire process we would be rewarded on Qualification Day with high scores."

Markel, already an experienced shooter, took the practice seriously and it paid off. "In my mind there was no other choice. As my primary marksmanship instructor had advised, on qualification day, my dedicated dry-fire work was rewarded with an expert rating, the highest rank awarded to Marines."

Marine or not, you should learn to master dry-fire practice with a handgun. It will pay off when you load the gun for live-fire practice or when it counts even more — when you need the handgun to defend your life.

Dry-Fire is for Everyone

As a Marine, Markel trained beside the "best of the best" in the military. He worked beside special operations personnel from the Marines, Army, Navy and Air Force.

"What they all have in common is not the amount of live-fire that they do," he said. "It's the amount of dry-fire. Many years ago, a friend offered a simple explanation. He told me the difference between an amateur and a pro is how much dry-fire they do."

Markel and other experts believe far too many shooters have the misconception that dry-fire is for beginners only. They perform dry-fire practice until proving they can handle a firearm safely with live ammunition. They advance to live-fire and never go back to dry-fire practice. "For those people, I would

offer the following advice," said Markel. "Max Michel and Todd Jarrett are two of the top competitive shooters in the world. During separate interviews, I asked them both about their thoughts on dry-fire practice. Each man related that when they made the decision to become a professional shooter, to do it for a career and use that money to feed their families, they started a dedicated regimen of dry practice."

He continued, "Max and Todd each stated they would spend two to three hours a day, six days a week on dry-fire practice. Todd related he did it two hours a day, six days a week, for the first 10 years."

Dry-fire practice is not just for beginners. Dry-fire practice is something you should practice your entire life as a shooter.

The Trap

If a down side to dry-fire practice exists, it is a misconception or misunderstanding that by simply holding a pistol and snapping the trigger, you are practicing. Without some kind of professional training or guidance, self-initiated dry-fire can lead to unsound gun handling and ingrained bad habits.

Ingraining bad habits through poorly applied dry-practice gives some instructors a reason to shy away from the practice or not recommend it. However, if instructors consider dry-fire with an open mind, they realize that the technique of dry-fire is not at fault in this equation, but rather the erroneous application of the technique. Just because a person fails to understand proper dry-practice does not mean the method itself is flawed.

Before you begin a regimen of dry-fire practice, you should attend a professional shooting course that reinforces marksmanship principles. Instructors should show you how to properly dry-practice and they should observe and ensure that you perform correctly.

Dry-Fire Beginning

Before using any firearm for non-firing training or practice, you must ensure the gun is unloaded. Two individuals should inspect the gun to confirm that it is unloaded and ready for dry-fire. You can then remove all live ammunition from the practice area, taking safety another step.

The following recommended dry-fire drills will help you improve accuracy and repetition of technique as you progress in your training.

Always check and recheck to make sure your weapon is unloaded before any dry-fire practice.

151

Coin Drill

One of the oldest dry-fire techniques or methods is the Coin Drill. Begin with an unloaded and cleared handgun. Point the handgun in a safe direction. Hold it as you would for live-fire. Have a partner place a coin on the top of the slide or frame. Attempt to dry-fire the gun without causing the coin to fall. Quarters and nickels are good to start. Move to pennies and dimes as your skill increases.

If you are able to complete the entire trigger press on a double-action pistol without disturbing the penny or dime, then you are well on your way to mastering the trigger press. For a real challenge, have a shooting partner balance an empty cartridge on the flat surface of your front sight if practical. Conduct this drill until you can balance the coin or case proficiently.

Reset Drill

Instructors designed this drill for semi-automatic pistols. A shooting partner greatly enhances this drill. Press your pistol out with two hands and aim at a spot on a wall. Focus on the front sight. Smoothly press the trigger until the sear releases and hold it. While you keep the trigger pressed, have your training partner reach up with one hand on the slide and the other on your shoulder.

Your training partner should then retract the slide all the way and let it go. After the slide cycles, ease the trigger out until you hear and feel the mechanical trigger reset. Press the trigger again and repeat the process five times. Switch positions with your training partner and repeat the process.

This drill provides an excellent way to learn how to use the mechanical trigger reset to your advantage. It also aids in learning how to operate older double-action and single-action pistols. It is possible to conduct this drill alone, but it is more beneficial if you hold the gun for both trigger presses.

Wall Drill

Many shooters have a difficult time disciplining themselves and forcing their eyes to focus on the front sight and not everything else in front of them. Teaching your eyes to focus intently on the front sight as you press the trigger is a skill that you must develop.

Using a twice-checked pistol, walk up to a blank wall. A plain white wall or some other single color works best. Avoid a backdrop that has any kind of pattern that might attract your eyes.

Draw your empty pistol and point it directly at the blank wall. Slowly move forward until the muzzle of the gun touches the wall and back up one inch. Now, focus intently on the front sight and press the trigger. Nothing remains in your field of vision other than your front sight. From a practical standpoint, your eyes cannot help but focus on the front sight – they have no other choice. This exercise will also help you verify proper sight alignment.

15: Live-Fire Practice

Practicing with your handgun generally falls into two major categories: live-fire and dry-fire. Both are valuable and mandatory for consistent proficiency. Repetition of learned skills is the key. Shooters who want the least expensive practice can accomplish that goal through dry-fire practice. This type of practice produces substantial repetition with no need for ammunition on a range. Training lasers and other aids allow for valuable aiming and trigger manipulation drills. You can accomplish all of this through dry-fire practice.

Live-fire practice is just as critical as it yields the ultimate integration of handling skills and testing weapon reliability. This gives shooters the best means for applying their ability to train for recoil, muzzle blast and target feedback.

Practicing with your firearm and ammunition is a necessity. It provides a confidence connection with your handgun. The trick lies in how that practice occurs.

Shooting your handgun should be fun. Going out with friends and family to share fellowship and fun is part of the game. Fun is indeed the name of the game, but it's not a substitute for practice.

From Training to Practice

Live-fire practice focuses on specific skills while using your handgun with live ammunition. Proper practice requires thought, structure and focus. Firing your handgun without these factors is merely shooting and not training.

As a rule, what we do in practice affects what we do in a life-threatening situation. Practice without thought can pattern real problems. In order to better yourself, you need to practice. That practice needs to have purpose.

The Purpose of Practice

The purpose of live-fire practice is hitting the target. Everything you do in live-fire practice should facilitate that goal. A shooter must properly aim the handgun, hold it on target and press the trigger. You should take all those steps as if occurring in a real-time, self-defense situation. In order for that to occur, you must safely and quickly bring the gun to use while keeping it loaded and running. Even more so, you should perform all these steps in stationary and moving positions.

Practice Process

Start your practice with accuracy drills that reinforce proper sight alignment, sight picture and trigger manipulation. Following your shot is one of the easiest methods for practicing and achieving the drill.

Starting at close range, take aim on a small target (two inches or less) and fire one shot. Follow that shot with the rest of the magazine, using your best accuracy skills. Try to put every round into the same hole. Do this slowly and pay close attention to proper aim, sight picture and a smooth trigger press.

The goal of this drill is to see any errors and correct them accordingly. If you have a partner, have them load some dummy rounds for you mixed with live rounds. Shooters will notice any anticipation of the round going off by a substantial flinch when firing the dummy round.

Practice this drill at various ranges out to 25 yards. Your mistakes become more evident as you move away from the target. Take time to address those shortcomings before moving.

Next, enlarge the target to no more than eight inches in diameter. Add body movement. Draw to a ready position, come up on target and fire. Directly draw and fire. Draw and then move. Repeat the process. Add simple and basic movements that correspond with your skill level. Shoot while moving and add barricades or barriers. Take your basic skills and add the real world. Speed is not an issue. Practice at a consistent pace where you can safely maneuver. Never rush during live-fire. Always move at a pace where you feel safe. Incrementally increase your speed, but only as you get better and more comfortable.

Speed and Tactical Loading

Use speed reloads for live-fire practice when rapid firing and accuracy are your goal. Follow this process for speed reloading with a semi-automatic pistol.

Begin with the slide in battery. Load a magazine with five rounds. Fire a round, then reload with the slide forward and fire again. Follow this process for reloads on a locked slide (locked to rear). Load a single round in the chamber. Remove the magazine and insert an empty magazine. Fire, reload and then get back on target and fire again. Focus on always hitting the target. You are training yourself to come off target, reload, get back on target and get hits.

In addition, practice with tactical reloads as your skills improve. Start from a ready position. Perform your preferred tactical reload. Go back to the ready position and then holster. Practice by coming up on target following the reload and firing.

These drills ensure your pistol is reliable and that it locks open on an empty magazine. You also learn where to hold and aim at various distances, which better prepares you for a real-world encounter.

Practice Primer

Start with these few simple exercises. With practice, your live-fire experience will thrive and encourage continued improvement. Depending on your skill level, you can make this more or less complicated.

Live-fire practice also ensures conservative use of ammunition, which is important for today's cost-conscious shooters. There is the added benefit of staying sharp for the entire training session. Fatigue leads to a loss of focus and delay in paying attention to detail. Neither shortcoming produces a safe scenario in a self-defense or concealed-carry environment.

Focused live-fire practice means your sessions are shorter. You fully engage for the entire session, thereby reducing the likelihood of accidents. The ultimate goal of practice is to learn, build or maintain a shooting skill.

16: Evaluation Exercises

Am I improving? Are my skills deteriorating? Dedicated shooters often pose these questions to themselves. If you are a coach or instructor, you might consider the same questions regarding your students. Are they improving, staying the same or losing their skills?

The act of employing a firearm, whether during deliberate competition, for recreational sport, hunting or to keep at the ready for personal defense, is both a mental and physical exercise.

Like any physical endeavor, such as golf, tennis, baseball, or basketball, after you learn the fundamentals, you must continually practice and challenge yourself to seek improvement. It's dumbfounding that some people believe by taking a single training session they have 'learned enough' to not only be proficient, but also have the ability to use the gun under high stress.

Consider the following questions. Would you lie down on the operating table and allow a surgeon who has only had one session of training to cut you open? Would you willingly get on an airplane with a pilot who took one session of lessons and has not flown a plane since that day ten years ago? Assuming that you are a thoughtful person, we will presume your answer to both questions is a resounding "no."

Defending your life and the lives of those you love from a sudden and violent attack is one of the most harrowing and stressful experiences you could ever experience. Amazingly, people will rarely, if ever, practice with a tool that they have set aside for the express purpose of saving their own life. However, considering you have this text in your hands, it appears you are a proactive person and genuinely seek improvement.

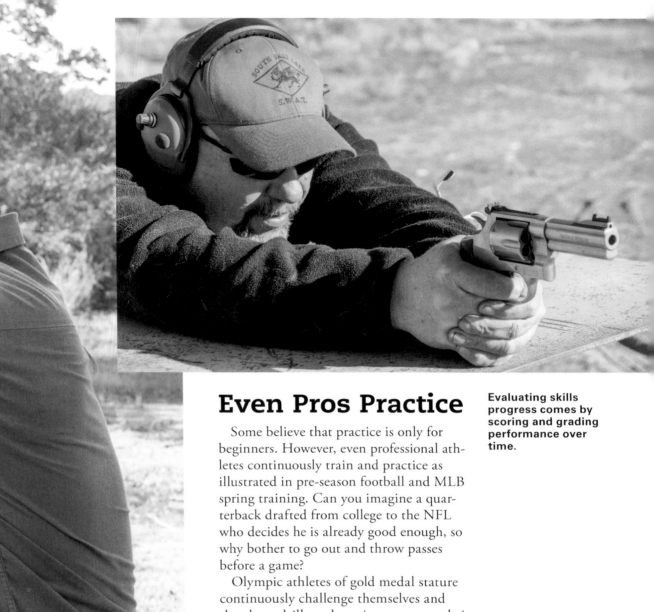

Even Pros Practice

Some believe that practice is only for beginners. However, even professional athletes continuously train and practice as illustrated in pre-season football and MLB spring training. Can you imagine a quarterback drafted from college to the NFL who decides he is already good enough, so why bother to go out and throw passes before a game?

Olympic athletes of gold medal stature continuously challenge themselves and they have drills and routines to gauge their progress. Gold medal winners don't settle for "good enough" and they don't have the nicest, most comforting coaches, as their coaches are generally hard-nosed, taskmasters.

Evaluating skills progress comes by scoring and grading performance over time.

161

Handgun Skill Maintenance

From a strict marksmanship standpoint, evaluate your skill by simply hanging a paper bull's-eye target out at a predetermined distance and slow-firing a set number of rounds. If the rounds fall inside the scoring rings and your total numeric score is higher today than it was last week, then you have improved.

This is generally as far as most shooters go with their evaluation drills. They shoot 10 or 15 rounds into a bull's-eye target. Then they eyeball the group and decide that they did or did not do better than the last time. This is not very scientific or reliable. Everyone has good and bad days. Some days you may feel like you are "on" and some days you do not.

If you are genuinely serious about seeking and tracking self-improvement and honestly evaluating your performance, then you should start by purchasing one simple item, a compact notebook. Yes, we live in a digital age, but a low-tech paper and pen setup keeps everything simple. If you wish to use your smartphone, go for it.

On day number one of USMC Rifle Training, the drill instructors issued a Rifle Marksmanship Data Book to every recruit in my platoon. This pocket-sized, spiral bound book included

marksmanship fundamentals and instructions on how to specifically adjust the front and rear sights on the M-16A2 service rifle. The book displayed images of sight alignment and sight picture, and included numerous logbook pages to record your practice and range sessions.

Each day that we went to the live-fire range, we recorded the date, time and weather conditions to include temperature, wind conditions and whether or not it was sunny, partly, cloudy, overcast, etc. All of these variables affect a rifleman's performance.

If you use an indoor range, the climate stays consistent from day to day. If you use an outdoor range, it might not be a bad idea to account for the weather conditions. Were you hot and sweaty or cold and fighting a strong headwind?

Regardless of the range situation, you should always record the date and time. Remember, we are trying to establish some type of baseline. You may find, over a period of several months, that you perform better when you go to the range early in the day or perhaps you do better in the evening. Regardless, the only way to evaluate your performance over weeks, months or years is to track it.

All it takes for the One Box Workout is
a single box of practice ammunition.

One Box Workout
Making the Most of
Your Practice Time

We referenced and discussed the One Box Workout as a baseline practice routine during the previous handgun fundamentals book. In its basic form, we don't put time constraints on the drills in the OBW. However, when it comes to self-evaluation and performance improvement, you can easily add the element of time or, more appropriately, time constraints to the formula as well as specific distance to the target.

Choose some type of paper or cardboard target that has either scoring rings or a delineated preferred zone. On the *Student of the Gun* official target, a thoracic triangle lightly outlines the chest to the head portion of the silhouette target. Every shot inside the triangle is a hit. Every shot outside of it is a miss. You can use an 8- or 12-inch bull's-eye or anything you like. The trick is to use the same target every session so you have an accurate comparison.

We have added a target distance and a baseline time limit for each portion of the OBW shooting drills. When it comes to keeping track of time, you can work with a range partner who has a stopwatch and whistle, or you can purchase one of several types of available shot timers. Naturally, a digital shot timer records your times much more accurately than a wristwatch, but these items do require a monetary investment. Expect to pay $100 to $200 for a quality shot timer.

If you have never run through the One Box Workout, it's best to shoot it first without any time constraints. Take your time and do it correctly before you try to go fast.

One Box Workout

Although this particular workout is designed for handgun shooters, one could adapt it for the carbine. We will begin with a single box of 50 rounds of training ammunition. You can purchase these from most every ammo maker. It is up to you if you wish to use more ammunition.

In order to get the most from your practice routine you should arrive at the shooting facility with a plan. You did not come to simply launch bullets down range and make noise.

The One Box Workout combines a baseline time limit with the target distance.

Step 1 - Two-Handed

We begin the first drill by loading ten rounds into the handgun. If your gun holds less than ten rounds, fill it to capacity.

With the target set at five to seven yards, begin with a two-hand hold and slow-fire your first magazine or cylinder. Take your time and focus on a smooth, deliberate trigger press and clear front sight. As a practice regime, this is not a speed drill, but rather, a fundamentals drill. However long it takes to place ten well-aimed shots on the target is the amount of time you will take.

Evaluation Exercise: Target at 7 yards, Time Limit - 10 seconds, Record all shots inside the preferred zone

Keeping the wrist locked is the goal of single-hand shooting.

Step 2 - Dominant Hand Only

Reload your handgun and repeat the first drill, only this time, fire all rounds using only your strong/dominant hand. We suggest taking your non-dominant hand and holding it close to your chest.

Again, take your time and focus on solid marksmanship fundamentals. One of the keys to success when shooting single-handed is to ensure your wrist is locked. Focus on the front sight as you fire each shot.

Evaluation Exercise: Target at 5 yards, Time Limit - 10 seconds, Record shots inside preferred zone

Step 3 - Support Hand Only

Continue your practice session. Reload your handgun and fire the next exercise using only your support or off hand. Focus intently on your front sight and ensure your trigger press is smooth and deliberate.

Remember to lock your wrist so the gun does not flail about. If you conduct this step of the workout with diligence and deliberation, it might surprise you how well you do with your non-dominant hand.

Evaluation Exercise: Target at 5 yards, Time Limit - 10 seconds, Record shots inside preferred zone

A slow, deliberate trigger press is the goal of the Support-Hand Only drill.

167

A slow, smooth draw of the gun from the holster is the purpose of the Holster Drill.

Step 4 - Holster Drill

We now move on to the holster drill. If your practice range forbids the use of a holster, simply set the gun on the little shelf or table and pick it up each time. Keep in mind, for the basic practice regimen, this is not a time drill. This drill is about performing it correctly, not fast.

With your handgun loaded and holstered, smoothly draw and engage the target. Fire two shots and then slowly and hesitantly re-holster. Never race back to the holster, GO SLOW. Repeat the drill until you empty the gun.

If you cannot use a holster, don't sweat it. Stage your gun on the stand or table as you keep it at the ready at home. Take a step back. On command, step forward, pick up the gun and fire two or three shots at the target. Reset and do it again.

Evaluation Exercise: Target at 7 yards, Time Limit - 3 seconds for 2 shots on target from the holster, 10 rounds total, Record shots inside the preferred zone.

Developing a repetitive and consistent process of loading magazines is the goal of the Loading Drill.

Step 5 - Loading Drill

Download your magazines to two, three or four rounds. Begin with a partially loaded handgun. Engage the target until the gun runs dry and then reload. Focus on performing in a very deliberate and methodical fashion. Repeat the drill two or three more times.

Evaluation Exercise: Target at 7 yards, Load 3 magazines with 3, 3 and 4 rounds. Begin with any magazine loaded into the pistol. Fire all ten rounds, reloading as you progress. Time limit - 20 seconds. Record shots inside of the preferred zone.

* This is more difficult if you use a revolver, but you can utilize speed-loaders or quick-strips. Add 5 seconds to the evaluation time.

The One Box Workout provides an excellent drill to use as a skill maintenance exercise. Adding a set distance and time factor allows you to use the OBW as a skill evaluation exercise. As with any type of evaluation drill, it is imperative to keep accurate notes. Be honest with yourself. The only one you will be cheating is yourself.

An electronic timer is a valuable tool for the Ten, Ten and Eight Drill.

Four, Ten, Four

The "Four, Ten, Four" evaluation drill is based on the previous drill. However, this drill requires multiple targets. Place two identical targets down range at 10 yards. The shooter begins with a 4-round magazine in the gun and a four round magazine in a magazine pouch.

On command, the shooter must place four shots into target A, reload the pistol and then put the four remaining rounds into target B. The time limit is 10 seconds. Record all the rounds in the preferred zone. This drill combines not only marksmanship under time constraints, but it also tests the shooter's ability to manipulate the pistol in an efficient manner.

Ten, Ten and Eight

The "Ten, Ten and Eight" drill was taught to me during a three day pistol and carbine course a couple of years ago. This evaluation exercise also requires some type of timekeeping method.

Place your preferred target down range at 10 yards. With your pistol loaded with 10 rounds of ammunition, begin in a standing ready position. On the command or signal, fire all 10 rounds into the preferred zone in a time limit of eight seconds. Record the shots in the preferred zone.

If your preferred handgun will not hold 10 rounds of ammunition, decrease the time limit by a one-half second per round subtracted. For example, an 8-round M1911A1 should have a time limit of seven seconds while a six shot double-action revolver should have a time limit of six seconds.

The Four, Ten, Four drill increases profiency with reloading the gun.

Parting Thoughts

Set realistic goals. Beware the temptation to shoot faster than your skill allows. Set in place a solid set of marksmanship and firearms handling skills before you attempt rapid shooting or multiple target drills.

Once your skills are solid, move on to evaluation drills and exercises. If you find yourself turning money into noise, put on the brakes and park the timer. Run through the previously described drills without time constraints. It is always a good idea to run through these drills off the clock first to understand the requirements.

After considering all of the aforementioned practice routines and evaluation exercises, you should understand that you don't necessarily need a high volume of fire to maintain skill or to evaluate it. For the cost of only 50 to 100 rounds, you can complete numerous exercises and reap far greater benefits than simply going to the range and mindlessly launching round after round. A shooter who dedicates themselves to a deliberate practice routine of 50 to 100 rounds will be far ahead of someone whose goal is to generate a big pile of empty brass.

With a baseline of data recorded over a few range sessions, you can start setting practical goals for yourself. Keep track of your shots and performance. If the drills become too easy, move the target out or shorten the time. You are the only limiting factor to how much you can achieve and how far you can go.

17: Parting Shot

This book starts by building a solid foundation of basic skills put into practice using the proper mindset. Building a foundation requires learning proven techniques such as accuracy, stability, balance and proper application. When combined, those techniques form the base.

Practiced to perfection, the basics will always serve you well in the real world. Advanced techniques are simply the basics expertly applied. Here is a recap of the basics covered in this book. Reread and study the content as you build on your foundation and become a more proficient shooter.

Gun-mounted lights are among the accessories that complete a well-supplied concealed-carry package.

Accessories

Choosing the proper equipment enhances your ability to apply the basics. Equipment should never serve as a substitute for basic skills. Guns and related accessories or aids will greatly assist you if you properly choose and apply these items. Aiming devices such as lasers, red dots and various sighting systems enhance your ability to properly align and see your sights. These devices get you in position and on target faster where conventional sighting proves difficult. Aiming devices give an edge when used properly and in the right environment.

Low and failing light conditions always exist without regard to your application. Whether in a restaurant, confined space or the dark of night, you should always have a light. You must properly identify the threat. It's as important as hitting the threat when required. In dim situations, your only choice is adding light to the threat and target area. A handheld light is equally important as spare magazines.

Weapon-mounted lights add another dimension to properly aiming under low light conditions. Facilitating a two-hand grip and maintaining the conventional shooting techniques increases accuracy. Weapon-mounted lights supplement a handheld light. It requires both to complete the light package. When used together, the lights provide incredible versatility, which enhances the ability to safely get the job done under low light conditions.

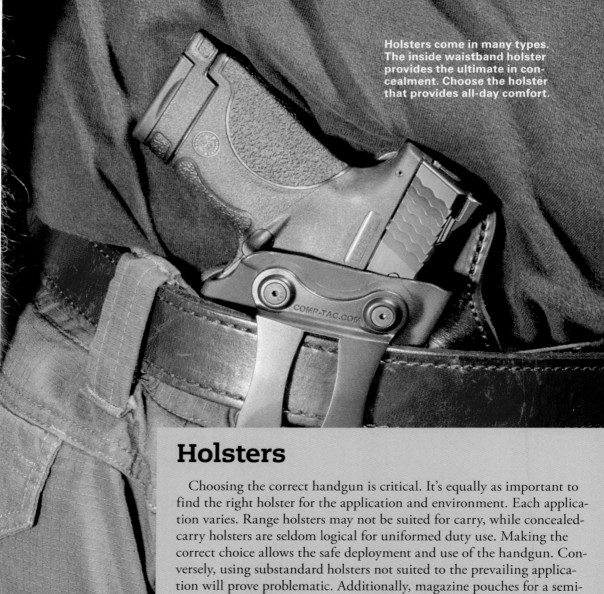

Holsters come in many types. The inside waistband holster provides the ultimate in concealment. Choose the holster that provides all-day comfort.

Holsters

Choosing the correct handgun is critical. It's equally as important to find the right holster for the application and environment. Each application varies. Range holsters may not be suited for carry, while concealed-carry holsters are seldom logical for uniformed duty use. Making the correct choice allows the safe deployment and use of the handgun. Conversely, using substandard holsters not suited to the prevailing application will prove problematic. Additionally, magazine pouches for a semi-automatic pistol or revolver are integral to this choice. Keeping a handgun running and loaded is critical to proper application. Choose the right pouches that facilitate proper loading techniques. The pouches should securely hold the magazines or speedloaders while allowing immediate access to ammunition while under stress.

To be successful, choose holsters, pouches and accessories that best support the application. Take adequate time to consider the recommendations in this book while seeking guidance from a gun shop or professional instructor. Having a good holster and the supporting items to go with it makes the overall shooting process more enjoyable and better applied under stress.

Training by a qualified instructor is the first step in learning intermediate shooting skills. Practice with dry-fire and then with live rounds is the next step toward becoming a skilled shooter.

Training and Practice

Once the equipment is in place, focus on proper training and practice. Learn the basics under the watchful eye of an instructor and during training. Shooters should begin with dry-fire and then practice what's learned in a live-fire situation. Repetition follows to form skills that can apply to real-world situations for self-defense.

When training, shooters should remain thoughtful, structured and practice with discipline and a solid focus. Structured practice leads to viable and usable skills. Quality training time yields improvement in the ability to apply skills. Evaluation drills determine if training equates to actual improvement.

Conclusion

Shooting a handgun with accuracy requires constant and consistent attention to the basics. Using a handgun in a self-defense or professional situation requires double the effort.

Proficient shooting is a perishable skill that fades with inactivity. Over the course of this book, the authors have tried to provide the basics necessary to achieve this process with the least amount of wasted time, effort and cost.

Establish a solid foundation, choose the correct equipment and spend quality time practicing proper use and application. We have done our best to give you the information to make the best possible choice for your needs while maintaining a solid focus on the basics.

Good shooting and be safe.

Appendix A: Manufacturers

A COMPILATION OF POPULAR HANDGUN MANUFACTURERS

Accu-Tek Firearms (Excel Industries, Inc.)
www.accu-tekfirearms.com
Excel Industries, Inc.
1601 Fremont Ct.
Ontario, CA 91761

American Derringer Corporation
www.amderringer.com
American Derringer Corp.
127 North Lacy Drive
Waco, TX 76705

Armscor USA and Rock Island Armory
www.armscor.net
Armscor USA and Rock Island Armory
150 North Smart Way
Pahrump, NV 89060

ATI (American Tactical Imports)
www.americantactical.us
American Tactical Imports
100 Airpark Dr.
Rochester, NY 14624

Beretta USA
www.berettausa.com
Beretta USA
17601 Beretta Dr.
Accokeek, Maryland 20607

Bersa (Eagle Imports, Inc.)
www.bersa.com
Bersa
1750 Brielle Ave, Unit B-1
Wanamassa, NJ 07712

Boberg Arms Corporation
www.bobergarms.com
Boberg Arms Corporation
1755 Commerce Court
White Bear Lake, MN 55110

Bond Arms
www.bondarms.com
Bond Arms Inc.
P.O. Box 1296
Granbury, TX 76048

Browning

www.browning.com
Browning
One Browning Place
Morgan, Utah 84050

Cabot Guns

www.cabotgun.com
Cabot Guns
799 N. Pike Road
Cabot, PA 16023

Charter Arms

www.charterfirearms.com
Charter Arms
18 Brewster Lane
Shelton, CT 06484

Christensen Arms

www.christensenarms.com
Christensen Arms
PO Box 240
550 N Cemetery Rd.
Gunnison, UT 84634

Citadel

www.legacysports.com
Legacy Sports International
4750 Longley Lane, Suite 209
Reno, NV 89502

Colt (Colt's Manufacturing Company)

www.coltsmfg.com
Colt Defense LLC
P.O. Box 118
Hartford, CT 06141

CZ-USA

www.cz-usa.com
CZ-USA
P.O. Box 171073
Kansas City, KS 66117

Diamondback Firearms, LLC

www.diamondbackfirearms.com
Diamondback Firearms, LLC
4135 Pine Tree PL
Cocoa, FL 32926

EAA (European American Armory)
www.eaacorp.com
EAA
P.O. Box 560746
Rockledge, FL 32956

Ed Brown Products, Inc.
www.edbrown.com
Ed Brown Products, Inc.
P.O. Box 492
Perry, MO 63462

FMK Firearms
www.fmkfirearms.com
FMK Firearms, Inc.
P.O. Box 1358
Placentia, CA 92871

FNH USA, LLC (FN Herstal)
www.fnhusa.com
FNH USA
P.O. Box 9424
McLean, VA 22102

Freedom Arms Inc.
www.freedomarms.com
Freedom Arms Inc.
314 Highway 239
Freedom, WY 83120

Glock, Inc.
www.glock.com
GLOCK, Inc.
6000 Highlands Parkway
Smyrna, GA 30082

Heckler & Koch
www.hecklerkoch-usa.com
Heckler & Koch
5675 Transport Boulevard
Columbus, GA 31907 USA

Hi-Point Firearms
www.hi-pointfirearms.com

Infinity Firearms
www.sviguns.com
Infinity Firearms
71229 Interstate 20
Gordon, TX 76453

I.O. Inc. (Inter Ordnance)
www.ioinc.us
I.O. Incorporated
2144 Franklin Drive NE
Palm Bay, FL 32905

Kahr Arms
www.kahr.com
Kahr Arms Factory
130 Goddard Memorial Drive
Worcester, MA 01603

Kel-Tec (Kel-Tec CNC Industries Inc.)
www.keltecweapons.com
Kel-Tec CNC Industries Inc.
1505 Cox Road
Cocoa, FL 32926

Kimber Manufacturing
www.kimberamerica.com
Kimber Mfg. Inc.
30 Lower Valley Road
Kalispell, MT 59901

Les Baer Custom Inc.
www.lesbaer.com
Les Baer Custom Inc.
1804 Iowa Drive
LeClaire, IA 52753

Magnum Research
www.magnumresearch.com
Magnum Research, Inc. Factory
12602 33rd Avenue SW
Pillager, MN 56473

Maximus Arms, LLC
www.maximusarms.com
Maximus Arms, LLC
1226-C Lakeview Drive
Franklin, TN 37067

Nighthawk Custom
www.nighthawkcustom.com
Nighthawk Custom
1306 W. Trimble Rd.
Berryville, AR 72616

Olympic Arms Inc.

www.olyarms.com
Olympic Arms Inc.
624 Old Pacific Highway SE
Olympia, WA 98513

Para USA, LLC

www.para-usa.com
PARA USA, LLC.
10620 Southern Loop Blvd.
Pineville, NC 28134-7381

Remington Arms Company, LLC

www.remington.com
Remington Arms Company, LLC
870 Remington Drive, P.O. Box 700
Madison, NC 27025-0700

Rossi

www.rossiusa.com
Rossi
16175 NW 49 Avenue
Miami, FL 33014

Ruger (Sturm, Ruger & Co.)

www.ruger.com
Sturm, Ruger & Co., Inc.
411 Sunapee Street
Newport, NH 03773

SCCY Industries

www.sccy.com
SCCY Industries
1800 Concept Court
Daytona Beach, FL 32114

SIG Sauer

www.sigsauer.com
SIG SAUER, Inc.
72 Pease Boulevard
Newington, NH 03801

Smith & Wesson
www.smith-wesson.com
Smith & Wesson
2100 Roosevelt Avenue
Springfield, MA 01104

Springfield Armory USA
www.springfield-armory.com
Springfield Armory
420 West Main Street
Geneseo, IL 61254

Steyr Arms (Steyr Mannicher)
www.steyrarms.com
Styer Arms
P.O. Box 840
Trussville, AL 35173

STI International, Inc
www.stiguns.com
STI International
114 Halmar Cove
Georgetown, TX 78628

Taurus International Manufacturing Inc.
www.taurususa.com
Taurus International Manufacturing Inc.
16175 NW 49 Avenue
Miami, FL 33014

Uselton Arms Inc.
www.useltons.com
Uselton Arms, Inc.
Franklin, TN 37064

Walther Arms
www.waltherarms.com
Walther Arms, Inc.
7700 Chad Colley Blvd
Fort Smith, AR 72916

Wilson Combat
www.wilsoncombat.com
Wilson Combat
2234 CR 719
Berryville, AR 72616

Appendix B: Organizations

A Girl and A Gun – A ladies only organization established by women shooters for women shooters with a passion for pistol, rifle and shotgun sports. The organization's mission is "to educate and encourage women about firearms usage, safety and promote women's shooting interest and participation in the competitive shooting sports."
www.agirlandagunclub.com

America's 1st Freedom – An official journal of the National Rifle Association that is focused on the constitutional right to keep and bear arms. America's 1st Freedom features the latest news concerning Second Amendment freedoms.
www.nranews.com/americas1stfreedom

American Handgunner – A magazine devoted to handguns, hunting, competition shooting, tactical knives and shooting-related activities that features reviews on guns, knives, ammunition, shooting gear, historical articles, self-defense and gun right information.
www.americanhandgunner.com

American Rifleman – A firearms publication owned by the National Rifle Association. The publication includes information on guns, newsletters, reviews, guides, galleries, video, blogs, training tips and top stories on guns.
www.americanrifleman.org

Collectors Firearms – A gun auction website with one of the largest collections of militaria, uniforms, weapons and memorabilia. Collectors Firearms features all kinds of antique and modern firearms.
www.collectorsfirearms.com

Civilian Marksmanship Program (CMP) – "The Civilian Marksmanship Program is a national organization dedicated to training and educating U.S. citizens in responsible uses of firearms and air guns through gun safety training, marksmanship training and competitions." With an emphasis on youth, the CMP Mission promotes firearm safety and marksmanship training.
www.odcmp.com

Combat Focus Shooting – A program that features handgun courses and instruction with a focus on real world defense scenarios. This shooting program is "designed to help the student become a more efficient shooter in the context of a dynamic critical incident."
www.combatfocusshooting.com

Concealed Carry Magazine – A concealed and carry publication featuring crucial advice for armed citizens to better protect themselves. Includes gun and gear reviews, life-saving training, tips and answers to concealed carry questions written by leading experts on self-defense and concealed carry. Concealed Carry Magazine is a publication of the United States Concealed Carry Association.
www.concealedcarrymagazine.com

Gun Broker – "The World's Largest Online Auction of Firearms and Accessories." Gun Broker provides a secure and safe way to purchase guns, hunting and shooting accessories, while promoting responsible gun ownership.

www.gunbroker.com

International Defensive Pistol Association (IDPA) – "The International Defensive Pistol Association is the governing body of a shooting sport that simulates self-defense scenarios and real life encounters." Founded in 1996, the IDPA was formed to appeal to shooters worldwide. The organization has more than 22,000 members, representing 50 countries.

www.idpa.com

International Practical Shooting Confederation (IPSC) – "The IPSC was established to promote, maintain, improve and advance the sport of IPSC shooting, to safeguard its principles and to regulate its conduct worldwide in order to cultivate safe, recreational use."

www.ipsc.org

National Rifle Association of America (NRA) – An influential American lobbying group and large supporter of the Second Amendment. Known as "America's longest standing civil rights organization." Formed in 1871 by Union veterans Col. William C. Church and Gen. George Wingate. The NRA sponsors marksmanship events and publishes firearm based magazines such as American Rifleman, American Hunter, America's 1st Freedom, Shooting Illustrated, Shooting Sports USA and NRA Insights.

www.nra.org

National Shooting Sports Foundation (NSSF) – Known as "the trade association for the firearms industry." The NSSF promotes, protects and preserves hunting and shooting sports.

www.nssf.org

NRA Insights – An NRA publication geared towards young shooters. The publication includes stories, gun safety, games, videos, tips and pointers.

www.nrainsights.org

Second Amendment Foundation (SAF) – Strong supporter of Second Amendment rights. Promotes firearm rights through educational and legal action programs designed to inform the public about the gun control debate.

www.saf.org

Shooting Illustrated – An NRA publication that highlights firearm news, weekly polls, tips, feature stories, blogs, videos, galleries, and firearm related gear.

www.shootingillustrated.com

Shooting Sports USA – An NRA publication that focuses on competition shooting news.

www.nrapublications.org/index.php/shooting-sports-usa

Shooting for Women Alliance (SFWA) – A nonprofit organization dedicated to educate women and youth worldwide about personal defense, firearms safety, conservation and enjoyment of the shooting sports.

www.shootingforwomenalliance.com

Springfield Armory Museum – From 1777 to 1968, the Springfield Armory Museum was the primary center for the manufacture of U.S. military firearms. "The Springfield Armory National Historic Site commemorates the critical role of the nation's first armory by preserving and interpreting the world's largest historic U.S. military small arms collection, along with historic archives, buildings and landscapes."

www.nps.gov/spar/index.htm

Tactical-Life – Owned by Harris Publications, Tactical-Life is an umbrella website for the following publications: Tactical Weapons, Guns & Weapons for Law Enforcement, Special Weapons for Military & Police, Rifle Firepower, Combat Handguns, Tactical Knives, Guns of the Old West and The New Pioneer.

www.tactical-life.com

The Sportsman Channel – A television channel designed for outdoor enthusiasts with a focus on hunting, shooting and fishing for entertainment and education purposes. Known as "the leader in outdoor TV for the American Sportsman."

www.thesportsmanchannel.com

United States Practical Shooting Association (USPSA) – "The premier competitive shooting organization in the world." The USPSA site offers a club finder, articles for competitors, a rule book, match announcements and top news about the organization.

www.uspsa.org

USA Carry – A leading concealed carry online resource featuring concealed carry articles, news and training. USA Carry also features a directory where users can discover firearm instructors, gun shops, ranges and gunsmiths.

www.usacarry.com

Women & Guns – A firearms publication for women that provides information on firearms, self-defense, articles, events seminars and training information for women.

www.womenshooters.com